To you, My Special Friend,

With heart-filled appreciation, I say thank you from the center of my soul. It is because of you that this book will take flight and began its journey from state to state, person to person and families everywhere. You have one of the first printed copies that has been released in the midst of this world wide pandemic. 2020 has been a year of challenges, but you are still here to tell God thank you.

Bishop Dr. Dexter L. Kilpatrick

Could You Be…

TRICKED
AND
TRAPPED

DR. DEXTER L. KILPATRICK

Could You Be...
TRICKED AND TRAPPED
Written By: Dr. Dexter L. Kilpatrick

Cover photograph by ©JohanSwanepoel, Adobe Stock

Book Completion Services Provided by:
TRU Statement Publications | www.trustatementpublications.com

TRU Statement
PUBLICATIONS
www.trustatementpublications.com
Truth. Reflection. Unity.

Unless otherwise stated, all scripture quotations of the Holy Bible have been taken from the King James Version (KJV)

MY DEEPEST APPRECIATIONS TO...

My Wife Brigitte,

> *He who findeth a wife findeth a good thing,*
> *and obtaineth favour of the LORD.*
> *Proverbs 18:22 KJV*

Brigitte, you are my biggest cheerleader, my teammate, a coach at times, and my best friend next to the Lord, our savior, Jesus Christ. When the Word speaks of a man finding a wife as one who finds a good thing and obtains favor with God, I believe I did so when I met you, a virtuous woman of God. As long as I live, I shall give my life to you as Christ gave his life for the church. Brigitte C. Kilpatrick, you are the greatest.

To my children, Déjà, Juwan, Brianne, Bobbie, and Alisa, who could have a greater set of children that are all anointed, chosen, and appointed by God to be leaders in life? I know it's not easy being a pastor's kid, or a PK as we call it, but each of you is growing into mature men and women of God. I know you each will continue to do great things in this life. My prayers are with you; do everything you can to please

God first, and He will open every door that is needed for you to be successful.

CONTENTS

PREFACE

What you have in your hand is not just another book to read, it is the key to your next move in life. Many have read books that have great titles and storylines, but the ingredients listed in the books are not scripturally sound or spiritually able to produce a change in the reader's life.

There are some people who can read up to four or more books in a week, but what are they getting out of those books beside a good murder mystery, a hot steamy love story, or even the latest pop psychology self-help tips.

Now don't get me wrong, reading is one of the best tools we have to increase our knowledge and understanding of matters pertaining to this life, but when all we are getting is hours of reading and no result, that scares me. In this book, you will likely find some of your very own life experiences discussed on some of the pages.

One of the most trying things a person can face in life is being trapped in the cages of life and feeling that the key to escaping is just out of arm's reach. *Tricked and Trapped* is a book that has been written to show you how to get your hands on the key that your adversary has taunted you with for so many years. You really don't have to stay in the shape that you are in; all one has to do is find out how to get the key and then use it to work you in your personal situations.

The Word of God is not just a book of *thou shalt* and *thou shalt nots*. It is a book spanning centuries that tells various stories of the lives of ordinary people. Their stories are told honestly, with good and bad choices clearly laid out for the reader. The Bible is a fantastic resource for anyone looking to escape their own bad situation, as the lives that are depicted often show people going through the same struggles we ourselves are experiencing.

In this work that I have compiled, I will be using various biblical accounts to illustrate a specific trap or trick and then using scripture and a bit of conventional wisdom to show how the hope for deliverance can become a reality. So, my friend, read this entire book and you will find out that YOU CAN BE FREE.

INTRODUCTION

Ever been in a place where you had been tricked by someone and it became a game to them but a drastic headache for you? There is not one person in this world that I know who enjoys being held hostage to anyone or anything, in which they have no idea how to get out of the stronghold. In this book, we will find out that there is always a way out of anything that we get ourselves into, but we have to know which direction to go in, in order to find the light at the end of the tunnel.

It is a fact of life that we will one day find ourselves in difficult and trying situations. However, what we often fail to see is that getting out of such circumstances is in fact quite simple, but we either do not have enough of the knowledge we need or faith to open the doors that are holding us back.

As we embark on the details of this book, the way out of emotional, physical, or mental traps will be revealed by the time we reach the last page. My desire is that you do not come to any conclusions until you have read the book in its entirety. Most times, we lose out on the meat of the book because we read a short version of it from the beginning and think we know everything else that will be said. Do yourself a favor and complete the book; it will do your heart great to know that you can be free from tricks and traps.

CHAPTER 1

Let Me Out, Let Me Out!

There hath no temptation taken you but such as is common to man: but God is faithful, who will not suffer you to be tempted above that ye are able; but will with the temptation also make a way to escape, that ye may be able to bear it.

1 Corinthians 10:13

Remember how we would get together and play the game hide and go seek in the house with your brothers and sisters, or with your cousins who came to visit from out of town? It would normally be on a day when it was raining outside, with the wind blowing and whispering through the air, and the trees whooshing as the winds pierced through the leaves.

"Can we go outside?" we would ask our parents, even though we knew what they would say.

They would give us the look and then say, "You all know it is raining, so there is no going outside today, so don't ask. If you want to play, we have plenty of toys in the back room, or else find something to do inside the house. I know you have all types of things you can do, so make the best out of being inside!"

Dad would raise his head and sternly say, "You don't need to be out there in this weather, anyway."

Immediately, someone would say with a loud voice, "Let's play hide and go seek!" which would then start everyone shouting, "Not it. Not it. Not It!" until the last person to say something was chosen to be it.

What did it mean to be the person who was *it*? Well, the one chosen to be it was the person appointed to go in a corner and count to a certain number that was agreed upon by the others. After counting to that certain number, the person would then seek to find all who were hiding. Eventually, this scene would almost always result in a predictable outcome.

After playing hide and go seek for a period of time, we would get bored with the game. Then one of the older cousins would decide to get together and play a trick on the younger cousins. They would tell them, "You go hide in the closet this time and I will hide somewhere else, because they never check this closet."

The younger person, being naïve and trusting, believed every word that came out of the older kid's mouth and would go into the closet giggling, happy, and appreciative that they were allowed to hide in the best hiding place. With the victim now in place, all the other kids who were part of this trick would spring the trap, locking the closet and laughing as the child screamed for dear life, "Let me out! Let me out! Let me out!"

We knew, just as well as they did, that no one could hear them screaming because everyone was busy listening to music, talking loudly, or would be preoccupied with their own conversations in the other rooms of the house. We would chuckle and laugh hard, watching them as they tried, time after time, to turn the doorknob, only to find out it was still locked tight.

After so long, when my cousins and I (Oops, did I just tell on myself? Oh, well!) got tired of listening to the shouting, whimpering, empty threats, and crying from distress, we would quietly unlock the door and then sneak away to watch and see how long they would remain in the closet, thinking they were stuck. Sometimes it would be an hour or two before they finally came out. Occasionally, one of the parents would ask us where our cousin was, and all the older kids would break out laughing because we knew they were still sitting trapped in a closet that was no longer locked.

One of our uncles or aunties would go to the closet and our little cousin would either be sitting there with tear streaks running down their face, or they had fallen asleep because they were mentally convinced that they were going to be trapped in this closet, away from everyone, for a long time.

"What are you doing in this closet and why didn't you just open the door and come out a long time ago?" one of the parents would ask.

With even more tears flooding in their eyes, they would reply, "Because they tricked me into going into the closet and then locked me in there! Every time I tried to get out, it was locked, so I stopped trying, and I was trapped in there all this time. If I would have known the door was finally unlocked, I would have gotten out, but I figured if I tried to open the door again, it would still be locked!"

Now this illustration is not meant to be a reminder of the cruelty of children, rather a very simple picture of how our own experiences can appear when viewed from the outside looking in. Imagine that it was you as a child in this situation. If only you had known the way of escape had already been made. You would have come out a long time ago. But you gave up trying to escape because repeated attempts had just resulted in failure. You felt it was just too hard to try again. Yet, after being released, you saw just how ridiculously easy it would have been to try to get out just one more time.

Now, look back on the different experiences you have had in this life. Are you able to see that there are some things in life you would not have had to endure if you would have just tried one more time? All those dark days and nights would have been over; those troubling nightmares would have become daydreams of purpose and possibilities, if only we knew to turn the knob once again.

Where does this leave us as a people?

There are some who still want to blame everyone else for the time they have spent locked down and bound to nothing, and there are those who still want to make excuses for being without. Yet all they had to do was take one more chance and see how easy it was to walk out of a situation that seemed to be a stronghold.

No temptation has overtaken you except such as is common to man; but God is faithful, who will not allow you to be tempted beyond what you are able, but with the temptation will also make the way of escape, that you may be able to bear it.

1 Corinthians 10:13 NKJV

The Bible clearly states in the above verse that not only are the trials and problems we face common to everyone, but God always provides a way of escape. It is not His desire for anyone to stay locked up. So, this is my question to you: why is it so hard to find and follow the planned and divine escape that is set before us?

Most times, we stay stuck and trapped in situations because we really do not have a genuine desire to be free from some things in life. We want to stay locked in the closet with someone else's husband or wife; we want to stay in the closet hiding the secrets that we don't want anyone to know about.

Sure, we cry and wish for freedom when the secrets begin to wear on our souls, and we see ourselves in truth as being entrapped. But how often do we look for solutions that allow us to feel free and yet also allow us to maintain our secret sins? Do we really want to come out of the closet we've been lured into, or is it an act?

I can remember visiting various prisons and speaking with a few men and women who had been locked up for a long time. I asked them the question, "What are you going to do when you get out of here? You've been here 30 years, so what's your plan?"

Many times, the first thing I would hear from their mouth is, "Man, I don't know, to be honest I'm scared to go out into the real world! I've been locked in this prison for so long, I have no clue of what to do next. I have no idea how to live in the outside world. I feel so institutionalized in my mind."

The truth of the matter is that this person is trapped in his/her mind. This person is afraid, frustrated, and full of fear; praying they can survive in a world that they have not been in for some 30-plus years.

"And the LORD spoke to Moses, Go to Pharaoh and say to him, thus says the LORD: Let My people go, that they may serve Me." Exodus 8:1 NKJV

When we read the account of God giving Moses the command to go to Egypt and tell Pharaoh to release the Israelites, I believe we can get lost in the simplicity of the events themselves. I think we all understand that Pharaoh is not just going to obey God and say, "Hey Moses, that sounds like a great idea! We'll see you all when you get back!"

We understand it was not God's plan to have the Israelites go into the desert for three days, have praise and worship service, and then return three days later to resume a life of slavery. No! He was determined to set them completely free. However, I believe we can fail to understand that it wasn't just the Israelites' physical freedom that God was intent on bringing about.

The children of Israel spent 430 years in Egypt, just how God told Abraham it would occur in Genesis 15:13. However, the Israelites weren't immediately thrusted into slavery; it was a gradual change. When they came into Egypt originally, they came as Joseph's family. Highly favored because of the connection of their brother Joseph, they had lands, flocks, food, and safety. They became complacent, comfortable, enjoying the pleasures of the land they were in, and forgetting the promise that God made to their forefathers, which was to give them their own land in Canaan. They even began to go after the idols and gods of the Egyptians. They strayed from the faith of their fathers.

The stay was supposed to be a temporary one, but they soon felt that this was to be their permanent home. And then they came into powerful rulers, who didn't know Joseph, and who forced the Israelites into slavery. The Israelites made it so easy for the leaders to do this. They were no longer a separated people; instead, they made themselves subject to the leaders and gods of Egypt. Not only this, but even though they were considered to be a great multitude by the leaders of Egypt, such a great number that Pharaoh ordered the death of all male babies, we never read where they rose up in force to overthrow their oppressors.

They saw themselves as belonging to Pharaoh, not as the people of God. In other words, they tricked themselves by forgetting *whose* they were, and the Word that God had spoken concerning them; instead, they became trapped in their circumstances due to their mindset.

We see the evidence of this even before Moses is given the charge by God. We read in Exodus 2:11-14 that Moses kills an Egyptian who was beating an Israelite slave. However, he was not received as a great champion by the people. The very next day, when he stops two Israelites from fighting each other, one of them angrily confronts him and demands to know who made Moses judge over them. Presumably, Moses' killing of the Egyptian is only known to the Israelite who he saved. We are then left with the impression that an Israelite told the Egyptian authorities what Moses had done, causing him to flee Egypt for his life.

Forty years later, Moses returns to Egypt with the Word of deliverance and power of God. In Exodus 4:30-31, we see Moses and Aaron calling the elders of the Israelites together, giving them the good news that God heard their prayers and sent Moses to deliver them. Moses and Aaron even do signs that convince the elders that what they are saying was true. We read the people believed their report and bowed their heads and worshipped. But then, in the very next chapter, we see that instead of freedom, the children of Israel's slavery are made even harder because of Moses and Aaron delivering to Pharaoh the command of God.

Pharaoh increased the demands on the slaves and beat their leaders. The leaders confronted Moses and Aaron, accusing them of turning Pharaoh against the people, and because of this, Moses runs to God asking God why He hasn't delivered them like He promised. God explains that this deliverance is going to be done with a strong hand and mighty works.

In other words, it was going to be a process and in the natural mind, this makes sense. You cannot undo four hundred and thirty years of bondage with the snap of your fingers. The people of Israel had allowed themselves to become so entrenched in slavery and idol worshipping that God had to command the children of Israel to come out of Egypt!

"And Moses spoke before the LORD, saying, "The children of Israel have not heeded me. How then shall Pharaoh heed me, for I am of uncircumcised lips?" *Then the LORD spoke to Moses and Aaron and gave them a command for the children of Israel and for Pharaoh King of Egypt, to bring the children of Israel out of the land of Egypt."*

Exodus 6:12-13 NKJV

(emphasis author's)

What follows this pronouncement is God's judgment poured out on the gods of Egypt. It is interesting to note that God does not make a difference between the children of Israel and the Egyptians until the fourth plague; the plague of flies is only sent upon the Egyptian homes and land; but why is this so?

The children of Israel's idolatry needed to be dealt with. Once they began to see that the gods they had adopted were not gods at all, but powerless images and ideas, they were able to see that there was a true God who was able to save and deliver them from their bondage. Then they began to believe in the possibility of their freedom. But the changing of their mindset was not going to be easy. Even after the last plague was carried out, and the Pharaoh ordered the children of Israel to leave Egypt, but they still accuse Moses of bringing them out to die when they become trapped between the Red Sea and the armies of Pharaoh.

They had seen terrible judgments poured out on the Egyptians, yet they still doubted God's deliverance. God split the Red Sea, and the people passed over on dry ground and God released the Sea and drowned their enemies, and the children of Israel lived happily ever after, never doubting God again, right? Mmm, no.

What actually happens is a seemingly never-ending account of doubts, grumblings, complaining, accusations, mumblings, and even outright revolt.

After everything God had done in Egypt, and even after all the various ways that He would go on to deliver and provide for them in the wilderness, the Israelite people still complained and longed for everything they used to have. They had been content, complacent, and comfortable in their bondage.

Some of us today, like the ancient Israelites, choose to focus on the past and grasp a hold of the hurts and pains we have been through instead of looking forward to our freedom, which we have been promised to us by our Lord and Savior, Jesus Christ.

When we constantly focus on the things behind us, we become victims of what I call a denial blockage. This blockage occurs in our lives because we never allow ourselves the opportunity to grab hold of the things that are in front of us, which we so deeply desire. One of the most frustrating things a person can go through in life is to stand right outside their door of promise and allow fear to stop them from going through that door of change. When we dwell in the past of defeat, sorrow, and even success, we can become a prisoner to unseen chains that control our thoughts, actions, and deeds on a daily basis.

In the *Burden of Freedom*, written by Dr. Myles Munroe, he states, "Freedom without responsibility is still bondage to a person." In this book, Dr. Munroe further explains that the Israelites badly wanted to be free from their slave masters, but once they became free, they saw that it was now on them to build their own houses, grow their own food, clean their own clothes, pay their own taxes, tend to their husbands and wives all day long, and cut down more trees than they could ever imagine. Could you imagine the mindset of these people, as they looked around at *who* was going to do *what* on the first day of their freedom?

Which one of us would be the responsible party to delegate a daily work schedule? I could see Moses now asking God, "Lord, now that we have crossed the Red Sea, Pharaoh and his army have drowned as we watched, and all these men have their own pride and ego's, what do we do now? I can't control all these people."

The Bonds of the Comfortable

On a daily basis, Moses had to deal with this large group of complaining people who refused to see the promises that God made to them and the miracles He had already performed. Every day, there would be shouts in the camp from the people saying, "Moses, we know you said that the

Lord God almighty sent you to deliver us from Egypt, but why did God bring us out here in the wilderness to die? If this was His plan, we could have stayed in Egypt where we knew that they would feed us at least and have a place to sleep!"

How do you stop the chatter of complaining voices when you are leading a host of people who won't trust that there is more to life than poverty and being in bondage to someone else? Israel's deliverance from everything they would be confronted with was already assured before they crossed the Red Sea. God has allowed them to experience the power that would be working for them as they witnessed the plagues dropped on their enemies by God.

I don't know about you, but if God brought me through all of what He took the Israelites through, I would have no problem trusting Him in the wilderness. The plagues sent on the Egyptians were not intended for them alone as a punishment; rather, these plagues were for the children of God to take note they were in good hands with God on their side.

When a person has been in bondage for so long, they will

find the negative in everything before seeing there is a possibility in all things. Let's look a little closer at some of the Israelites' complaints. Their complaining started at the Red Sea as they saw the impenetrable expanse of water in front of them and heard the wheels of the Egyptian chariots echoing in the canyons as they bore down on them. The Word tells us that Moses told the people to not fear but watch and see the deliverance that God will bring about. Yet, apparently, even Moses experiences some misgivings, as we see in Exodus 14.

"And the LORD said unto Moses, wherefore criest thou unto me? Speak unto the children of Israel, that they go forward: But lift thou up thy rod, and stretch out thine hand over the sea, and divide it: and the children of Israel shall go on dry ground through the midst of the sea."

Exodus 14:15-16 KJV

Why would God, seemingly, rebuke Moses for praying about being blocked in and trapped on every side? When we read the beginning of the chapter, God tells Moses exactly what was going to happen; the Egyptians were going to be hardened by God and sent to pursue the Israelites. God had already promised He was going to deliver. However, what we saw is a common human phenomenon. Even though Moses knew God was going to work and save them, he became caught up in the people's doubt and fear.

How many of us have a friend, or multiple friends, who are negative or always have some sort of drama going on in their lives? How many times have we allowed ourselves to get caught up in their bad mind sets instead of holding on to what we know to be the truth? Moses allowed himself to, momentarily, slip into fear.

We can imagine his prayer to God, "Lord! I don't know what to do from this point; we have mountains on both sides of us, the sea is in front of us, Pharaoh and his army are approaching fast from behind us, and we are stuck in between a rock and a hard place!"

Seen with natural eyes, his situation could not have been worse. Not only are the Egyptians closing in on them, but now the people are beginning to panic and some figure that Moses brought them out to die. The Word says that some thought if they were taken back as slaves, it would be better than being dead. I imagine there were even others who probably started thinking that if they killed Moses, then maybe the Egyptians would forgive them and let them return safely to their former homes and servitude.

Moses was sure God had spoken to him and told him to speak to Pharaoh. He was sure it was the hand of God who both brought the plagues on the Egyptians, and who delivered the people from their bondage with such a strong hand. But because he did not guard the truth of God's Word and ignored everything he saw and heard around him; he almost allowed the situation to get out of hand. God had to put him in check, and He had to do it quickly, because Moses' doubt would quickly infect the people and could have stopped this deliverance before it even started.

Moses' doubts would have reinforced the people's fears to such a point that no matter what he said to them, they would have just waited for the Egyptians to swoop down on them, and they would have surrendered. When one has made up in his/her mind that there is no way out of a situation, there is very little you can say to that person to convince them otherwise. At the time of being challenged, they quickly tell themselves that the end has come for them, and they would rather imagine sickness, death, and defeat than to see deliverance and freedom.

Moses, then having heard God's orders clearly, springs into action and follows the command of God.

"And the angel of God, which went before the camp of Israel, removed and went behind them; and the pillar of the cloud went from before their face, and stood behind them: And it came between the camp of the Egyptians and the camp of Israel; and it was a cloud and darkness [to them], but it gave light by night [to these]: so that the one came not near the other all the night. And Moses stretched out his hand over the sea; and the LORD caused the sea to go [back] by a strong east wind all that night, and made the sea dry [land], and the waters were divided. And the children of Israel went into the midst of the sea upon the dry [ground]: and the waters [were] a wall unto them on their right hand, and on their left.

Exodus 14:19 - 22

We see then that when God comes to deliver, He comes to deliver everyone who believed He could. In Mark 9:23, Jesus himself said the same to the father of the boy possessed by demons, "Jesus said unto him, if thou canst believe, all things [are] possible to him that believeth."

Being set free from bondage is all based on what your desires are. If you really want it, then you have to go after it just as the woman with the issue of blood, who was bound for 12 long years. Mark 5:25 tells us that this Gentile woman had done all she could for herself, but when she got to the point where she became tired of being a victim of sickness, she launched out in faith and said to herself, "If I could but touch the hem of his garments, I would be made whole."

The writer, Mark, says that this woman saw Jesus and pushed, forced, fought, and fashioned her eyes on Him, paying no attention to anyone else until she reached out and touched the hem of His garment. The Bible explains that it was at that very moment she was made whole as the virtue left Jesus' body, breaking her chains of bondage forever.

Again, my question to you is "How bad do you want it?" In order to get what God has for you in this life, it is mandatory that you free yourself from the past and start pressing forward and moving towards your promised future. Tomorrow is not a distant dream or baseless hope, it is right around the corner from where you are, right now. But you have to believe in your heart, soul, and with all your strength that God is not only willing to free you and give you all that you need to reach His plan for your life, but He is in fact eagerly waiting and looking for those who do not stop in their pursuit of Him or in their belief in Him.

"But without faith it is impossible to please Him, for he who comes to God must believe that He is and that He is a rewarder of those who diligently seek Him,"

Hebrews 11:6 KJV

Are you seeking God for freedom from the traps of this world, or do you still believe that there is no way out for you in life? There is more to life than past bondages, hurts, failures, and disappointments; as long as you have breath in your body, you must look for, and believe in, the way out. God is and will always be the way maker for His people.

CHAPTER 2

The Mouse Trap of Life!

Blessed is the man who endures temptation; for when he has been approved, he will receive the crown of life which the Lord has promised to those who love Him. Let no one say when he is tempted, "I am tempted by God;" for God cannot be tempted by evil, nor does He Himself tempt anyone. But each one is tempted when he is drawn away by his own desires and enticed.

James 1:12-14 KJV

Imagine, for a moment, in your house is a small annoying mouse that only comes out when you have company. It's as if it waits for the most inopportune time to show itself to your visitors. You could be watching television, eating dinner, or just shooting the breeze with your best friends and then all of a sudden that little critter shoots across the foot of the person who is most afraid of mice.

Imagine the chaos that follows. People are running, screaming, jumping on furniture, and climbing up the walls.

The house looks as though a catastrophic bomb has been dropped on it. You are so upset, because not only has your house been left in extreme disarray, but the enjoyable time you were supposed to be spending with friends and loved ones has been ruined. And even worse, it is likely that your friends are not coming back to visit anytime soon; even when you tell them you are going to go out, right away, and get the biggest and best mouse trap money can buy. You can see in their eyes they will not feel safe enough to visit for quite a while. And now you fear if word gets out (as it generally does) that you have a mouse problem, you are probably going to find your social calendar opening up pretty quickly.

When I grew up, we once had a problem with a mouse in the house. We used to chase that mouse all around the house with brooms and sticks trying to kill him, but he would always get away, usually right when we thought we had the thing trapped in a corner. One experience in particular stands out in my memory. Everyone in the room saw the mouse run behind the couch. Immediately, we each grabbed our weapons of war; the living room was instantly under tactical alert. I remember thinking, "This is it; this is the day he dies."

I stood on one side of the couch; my sister stood on the

opposite side. My mom was standing facing the couch while looking for a place to run if it came her way. One of my cousins had found a large box and was holding it in his hands, ready to throw the box over the mouse in order to catch it before it could escape our ambush. My sister and I agreed to move the couch on the count of three, and from there, launch a head on attack. "On the count of three; 1...2...3!" We moved the couch, the mouse took off running one way, and we all ran the other way, leaving our weapons in the middle of the floor. With the first brilliant attempt at a failure, we decided on the next step to catching this mouse— "Let's go buy a trap!"

Now, pay close attention to everything I say from this point, because this is how Satan traps us as individuals when we are ignorant of his devices and schemes. My cousin and I went to the store and bought the biggest trap we could find. However, once we got it to the house, we realized we didn't need to use a huge trap to catch a small mouse. In fact, the size of the trap would hinder us; not only would it miss the mouse by a mile, but it seemed we would be caught in the trap before anything else, because the trap was so big and bulky. Having finally come to our senses, my cousin and I went back to the store and purchased a more convenient trap, a small compact trap with a great amount of force behind it.

You see, it's not the big things in life that Satan traps us with. Instead, it's small traps that capture us. How? It's in the bait. It is not the trap that draws the mouse away from his hiding place; it's the bait used to set the trap that lures it out. Let's look at the way Satan uses our desires to lure us into his traps, which are set out for us.

"Man is drawn out, and drawn away by his own lustful desires,"

James 1:14 KJV

Have you ever watched one of those cartoons where the mouse is in his own little resting place where he made his home inside the walls of a certain house? I remember one cartoon where this mouse is sitting in his lazy boy chair and watching the television show that the owner of the house was watching; he had a small glass of fruit drink and was relaxing like a king. The cartoon goes on to show this owner of the house trying to catch this mouse, so he puts this trap down on the floor and stacks a nice large piece of cheese on the trap. The aroma of the cheese travels through the house and goes directly to the hiding place of the mouse. Next, you see the mouse, as he is driven closer and closer to the trap, being hypnotized and drawn away from his safety net by the smell of cheese sitting in the middle of the trap.

The Smell of Food

Many of us have found ourselves in the very position that Mr. Mouse is in now. Think about the new year's resolution you made to lose a little weight by not eating sweets anymore. You wake that next morning pumped up for work; you tell yourself that this is the first day of your change in life. You start the car and begin listening to the radio, when all of a sudden that smell of fresh donuts, cake, cinnamon rolls, apple fritters, or glazed twisters hit your nose with a taste of coffee, and you find yourself in line getting a dozen donuts; promising yourself you will start fresh tomorrow, and this will be your last cheat day.

Well, what happened between you leaving home and getting to work? Yes, that's it! You were drawn away from your plans by the lust of your flesh; your desire took control of your goals and aspirations. Don't feel bad, you are not alone in this case. Many people do worse things every day and tell themselves that this will be the last time they do it.

The effects of cheese on a mouse is something to watch. Remember, the mouse was minding his own business until the smell came into his hiding place. It's easy for us, as a people, to hide from sinful desires when we are always around praying saints, but it is another thing to try and fight off this feeling when you are surrounded by other people who love to do the things you are trying not to do.

The Smell of Drugs

Those who have fought drug addictions will tell you that a person who has been clean from drug use for a period of time can easily be drawn back into it, just by smelling the aroma of the preferred drug. The only way to escape the lure of falling back into using is to remove themselves from the areas in which the odor resides. Those who do fall off the wagon, so to speak, almost always claim the same thing: "I wasn't strong enough."

I did an interview with a very close friend of mine who had been strung out on drugs for a very long period of her life (to protect the names of the innocent, we will refer to her as "Not Strong Enough"). There was a time when she would be so high on drugs, we thought she had overdosed. On several occasions when we found her in the streets or outside a dope house, we were sure she had gone to meet her Maker. During her interview, she told me that the hardest part of staying clean was staying out of its reach. She said, "As an addict, you don't have to go looking for the drug. It comes looking for you and it knows just where to find you at any time, and it will surely find you out."

During our interview, her eyes would begin to water as she expressed her fear of ever having to face those times and trials of life again. After really looking back on her life, Mrs. Not Strong Enough started to give God, the Father in heaven, praise for delivering her from death and bondage, so many times over.

Personally, I can think back on the times when my mother would ask this woman, "Why do you do this? What is it that makes you keep going back and leaving your kids for days at a time? What is so important about something that leaves you half to almost dead that you keep running to?"

She would always say to my mother, in a very soft voice filled with tears, "Carol, I can't stop, and I want to, but nothing helps. I've tried this and I've tried that, but nothing is working for me."

But my mother never gave up on her. She would attempt to "detox" her right in our house. After every single time, she relapsed and went back to drug abuse. It was not the taste of the drug on her tongue that she was fighting. If the drugs were in her mouth, the fight was already over. What she had to fight, when she was clean, was the smell that lurked through the air. The smell would cause her to climb out of the window and sneak away from the house. She would find herself sitting amongst the addicts all over again, contaminating her inner man with the substance she knew would one day kill her.

Can anyone put fault on her alone? No! Her desires had her bound to the addiction; no matter how bad she did not want to use again, she did. One thing she said that scared her every day as she woke, was the knowledge that although she had fought with everything she had, she realized she would always be challenged with this deadly, mind-blowing demon on a daily basis. She feared that no matter how strong her desire was to stay clean and free; the addiction proved stronger than her determination.

Paul describes this struggle in Romans 7. When he said that whenever he willed to do good, evil was always present to challenge his good deeds.

7 What shall we say then? Is the law sin? God forbid. Nay, I had not known sin, but by the law: for I had not known lust, except the law had said, Thou shalt not covet. 8 But sin, taking occasion by the commandment, wrought in me all manner of concupiscence. For without the law, sin was dead. 9 For I was alive without the law once: but when the commandment came, sin revived, and I died. 10 And the commandment, which was ordained to life, I found to be unto death. 11 For sin, taking occasion by the commandment, deceived me, and by it slew me. 12 Wherefore the law is holy, and the commandment holy, and just, and good.

13 Was then that which is good made death unto me? God forbid. But sin, that it might appear sin, working death in me by that which is good; that sin by the commandment might become exceeding sinful. 14 For we know that the law is

spiritual: but I am carnal, sold under sin. ¹⁵ For that which I do I allow not: for what I would, that do I not; but what I hate, that do I. ¹⁶ If then I do that which I would not, I consent unto the law that it is good. ¹⁷ Now then it is no more I that do it, but sin that dwelleth in me. ¹⁸ For I know that in me (that is, in my flesh,) dwelleth no good thing: for to will is present with me; but how to perform that which is good I find not. ¹⁹ For the good that I would I do not: but the evil which I would not, that I do. ²⁰ Now if I do that I would not, it is no more I that do it, but sin that dwelleth in me.

²¹ I find then a law, that, when I would do good, evil is present with me. ²² For I delight in the law of God after the inward man: ²³ But I see another law in my members, warring against the law of my mind, and bringing me into captivity to the law of sin which is in my members. ²⁴ O wretched man that I am! who shall deliver me from the body of this death? ²⁵ I thank God through Jesus Christ our Lord. So then with the mind I myself serve the law of God, but with the flesh the law of sin.

Romans 7:7-25

No one desires to be trapped in these issues of life. I believe anyone would say, if given the choice, they would choose to live a clean and good life. However, as Paul illustrated, we are living in a state of warfare between what we know to be

THE MOUSE TRAP OF LIFE!

right and good, and what our flesh desires to do. The constant tug of war happens to all of us every day, as our conscious choices are put to the test.

In Galatians 5:16, Paul admonishes us as believers to, "Walk in the spirit and we will not fulfill the lust of the flesh, for the flesh lust against the spirit, and the spirit against the flesh continually, so that you would not do the good you desire."

Every day when you wake up, you will awaken to another day full of challenges. My friend, it is up to you to consciously make the right choices for your future. As I have pointed out, smell can be very dangerous; for not only the person addicted to food but also to the person who admires the smell of a certain drug, which includes marijuana, crack, speed, cocaine, heroin, etc. It all leads to destruction and distractions.

Satan uses many "smells" to lure us back into sin. Memories of past sinful pleasures, chance meetings with old acquaintances, stressful situations, even loved ones and family members can be the bait the enemy uses to draw us back down into the depths of bondage. The only way we can escape these lures is to clear the area. When we recognize that a person or a situation is likely to lead us to fall again, we need to turn and run the other way. We cannot allow ourselves to worry about hurting the other person's feelings; if that person is the equivalent of poison, you need to escape.

Who knows, by taking that step and avoiding them and the situations that surround them, you might just help them find freedom one day. Oftentimes, when we see that others who we love are avoiding us because of the lifestyle we live, it can motivate us to want to change.

RESOLVED: Well, you may ask the question, *how do I keep myself from falling into the traps of the enemy?* Being that the Bible says a man is drawn away by his own lustful desires, it is up to you to keep your mind focused on the things of the lord. In order not to be drawn into a trap of the enemy, one must not let his/her senses be the driving force of all their decisions. Pray about everything. Talk to God about every decision that you will make when it comes to people, places, or things.

Remember, it's not the size of the cheese that draws you out of your safety zone, it's the smell of it. Be aware of your senses; touch, taste, smell, seeing, and hearing.

PRAYER: Dear Father, it is my prayer that you keep your eyes and your hands upon those who have read this chapter. Lord, we know it is so easy to be drawn away by our own lustful desires. So, I asked you, God, in the name of Jesus, that you would just hold us close to you; keep us in your will. Father God, keep the minds of those who are reading this steady on you.

Lord, there is nothing more that we can ask for than for you to show us the devil from far off. Lord, allow us to see his tricks, and his lies that he so strategically plans for us, each and every day. Allow us to see out of your eyes, and to understand everything that is either for us or against us, in Jesus' name. Amen!

TESTIMONY: After reading this particular chapter of this phenomenal book, I will say that my papa, Bishop Dr. Kilpatrick, really hit the nail on the head. All I can say at this time is that this chapter has caused me to think back to where it is that I've come from. It has reminded me that it's not always the size of the cheese that can grab my attention, but it's the enticing aroma of the cheese.

So many times, in my life, I was drawn out of my safe haven by manipulation and misleading words. For example, I remember being connected to different people who used a variety of different things, such as clothes, shoes, and empty promises of positions, to draw me into their conniving snares. At the very moment I was to be moved into the promised job title, or to operate in a so-called higher level of prestige, these heartless leaders would begin to snatch everything from up under me. So many times, I can remember being told that I had to start all over again.

Amazingly, it wasn't until I came to myself and realized that with or without the cheese, I could make it! After reading this book, I'm so grateful, and I believe it's going to help so many people who struggle with this type of issue on a daily basis. Thank You, Jesus, that the healing started with me.

Thank you, Dr. Kilpatrick.

Pastor Jermaine Lee Tim's

CHAPTER 3

There's No Light at The End
of The Tunnel

Is there truly a light at the end of every tunnel, or is this just something that we tell ourselves? Something that helps us to believe there's hope in order to make it easier to face challenges in life.

The Greek philosopher Plato along with Socrates posed this question to the world...

Stuck in a Cave

[1][*Socrates*] And now, I said, let me show in a figure how far our nature is enlightened or unenlightened: —Behold! Human beings living in a underground cave, which has a mouth open towards the light and reaching all along the cave; here they have been from their childhood, and have their legs and necks chained so that they cannot move, and can only see before them, being prevented by the chains

---

[1]Plato, The Republic, Book VII. Public Domian

from turning round their heads. Above and behind them a fire is blazing at a distance, and between the fire and the prisoners there is a raised way; and you will see, if you look, a low wall built along the way, like the screen which marionette players have in front of them, over which they show the puppets.

[*Glaucon*] I see.

[*Socrates*] And do you see, I said, men passing along the wall carrying all sorts of vessels, and statues and figures of animals made of wood and stone and various materials, which appear over the wall? Some of them are talking, others silent.

[*Glaucon*] You have shown me a strange image, and they are strange prisoners.

[*Socrates*] Like ourselves, I replied; and they see only their own shadows, or the shadows of one another, which the fire throws on the opposite wall of the cave?

[*Glaucon*] True, he said; how could they see anything but the shadows if they were never allowed to move their heads?

[*Socrates*] And of the objects which are being carried in like manner they would only see the shadows?

[*Glaucon*] Yes, he said.

[*Socrates*] And if they were able to converse with one another, would they not suppose that they were naming what was actually before them?

[*Glaucon*] Very true.

[*Socrates*] And suppose further that the prison had an echo which came from the other side, would they not be sure to fancy when one of the passersby spoke that the voice which they heard came from the passing shadow?

[*Glaucon*] No question, he replied.

[*Socrates*] To them, I said, the truth would be literally nothing but the shadows of the images.

[*Glaucon]* That is certain.

[*Socrates*] And now look again, and see what will naturally follow if the prisoners are released and disabused of their error. At first, when any of them is liberated and compelled suddenly to stand up and turn his neck round and walk and look towards the light, he will suffer sharp pains; the glare will distress him, and he will be unable to see the realities of which in his former state he had seen the shadows; and then conceive someone saying to him, that what he saw before was an illusion, but that now, when he is approaching nearer to being and his eye is turned towards more real existence, he has a clearer vision, -what will be his reply? And you may further imagine that his instructor is pointing to the objects as they pass and requiring him to name them, -will he not be perplexed? Will he not fancy that the shadows which he formerly saw are truer than the objects which are now shown to him?

[*Glaucon*] Far truer.

[*Socrates*] And if he is compelled to look straight at the light, will he not have a pain in his eyes which will make him turn away to take and take in the objects of vision which he can see, and which he will conceive to be in reality clearer than the things which are now being shown to him?

[*Glaucon*] True, he now.

[*Socrates*] And suppose once more, that he is reluctantly dragged up a steep and rugged ascent, and held fast until he's forced into the presence of the sun himself, is he not likely to be pained and irritated? When he approaches the light his eyes will be dazzled, and he will not be able to see anything at all of what are now called realities.

[*Glaucon*] Not all in a moment, he said.

[*Socrates*] He will require to grow accustomed to the sight of the upper world. And first he will see the shadows best, next the reflections of men and other objects in the water, and then the objects themselves; then he will gaze upon the light of the moon and the stars and the spangled heaven; and he will see the sky and the stars by night better than the sun or the light of the sun by day?

[*Glaucon*] Certainly.

[*Socrates*] Last of he will be able to see the sun, and not mere reflections of him in the water, but he will see him in his own proper place, and not in another; and he will contemplate him as he is.

[*Glaucon*] Certainly.

[*Socrates*] He will then proceed to argue that this is he who gives the season and the years, and is the guardian of all that is in the visible world, and in a certain way the cause of all things which he and his fellows have been accustomed to behold?

[*Glaucon*] Clearly, he said, he would first see the sun and then reason about him.

[*Socrates*] And when he remembered his old habitation, and the wisdom of the cave and his fellow prisoners, do you not suppose that he would felicitate himself on the change, and pity them?

[*Glaucon*] Certainly, he would.

[*Socrates*] And if they were in the habit of conferring honors among themselves on those who were quickest to observe the passing shadows and to remark which of them went before, and which followed after, and which were together; and who were therefore best able to draw conclusions as to the future, do you think that he would care for such honors and glories, or envy the possessors of them? Would he not say with Homer?

Sounds pretty familiar, huh? We see this kind of reaction in our family members, friends, fellow employees, and church members. Some people just have a hard time believing that there is more to their life than shadows.

How would you react; what would be your response to such an event? It's easy to say the right thing now, but when you are the one in the middle of the test, fear grips you just as it did those who are birthed and raised in darkness and shadows.

RESOLVED: One must remember that everybody in life will not appreciate the help, the hope, or the heroics that you may bring to them. As it was, the people would rather kill the man who brought the information back to them, because they did not believe there was a light at the end of the tunnel.

The Bible tells us that man would rather believe a lie than the truth, so always keep your head in the right direction. If God said there's light at the end of your tunnel, then look for it; walk into it as long as you have it. Continue to believe and share the truth about God and about our lives. Resolve!

PRAYER: Dear God, I am praying for each and every person who reads this chapter. God, understand that when people don't believe you, it does not mean that the truth is not real. Lord help your people to continue sharing that you are the light of the world and the light at the end of the tunnel.

Father, allow them to trust you where they cannot *trace* you and believe you when unbelief is stronger. We love you and we cherish you for everything that you will give us in the Life to Come. You are the light of our world.

TESTIMONY: After Reading this chapter, I was reminded of a very important time in my life. Years ago, I was in a legal battle involving, let's just say, a family member, and I had just given my life to Christ about 4 months prior. Without warning, that family member was injured and taken away. The police said another member of the family and I were at fault and we caused the accident on purpose!

I was devastatedly in disbelief. I'm not a liar, nor a criminal, but this was now my experience. It seemed the louder I said, "I'm innocent!" the stronger others said, "Guilty!"

So, I went to church looking for all my problems to be

solved right away. I got saved so life would be better, but it seemed to get worse. Pastors prayed, "The devil's busy." Evangelists, Mothers, etc. prayed the same prayers too.

"Bring her out Lord! No weapon form against her will prosper." Surrender, trust God, and more of the typical holiness prayers of deliverance and miracles, but nothing they prayed came to pass.

I kept going to church; they kept praying, but nothing changed. I was guilty before proven guilty. "Can God do something?" I was better off in the world unsaved! I began to get angry. "Why even go to church if God can't turn it around today?"

Because of the legal matter, I was required to attend court, psychiatric therapy, anger management, etc., etc. Every time I went to court, there was no resolution. I became depressed, began drinking again, suffered from anxiety, and I stopped going to church entirely.

The saints started coming to my house. Oh Lord. The same people, same prayers, and same tongues. I'm innocent of what I've been accused of and no one believes me. "Take away that stony heart. It's all working together for your good. Your miracle is on the way."

Nothing had changed and deliverance didn't come. No praise party for me. I was done. I was tired of scriptures, God, fasting, and praying. I decided I didn't want any more God stuff around me. This was not for me after all.

Then, an Evangelist (now my Godmother♥) invited me to a Revival that Friday night, and insisted that I go. I had gone to court 11 times and each time the answer was, "No, not yet, not enough evidence." So, I went to the Revival and rejected every bit of God that night. The topic was "How Long Will You Be Caught Between Two Decisions. You Either Believe God or You Don't!"

By the end of the Revival, I was Born Again and a believer in the Lord Jesus and His Mercy, Grace, and Power. That night was the 1st time the Lord God spoke directly to me. I couldn't believe that even though I rejected the scriptures, the prayers, the Word, and the men and women of God, God was still giving me a way out, another chance, and a choice. He Showed me His love.

The preacher said, "Always remember, whether God does it or not, remember He's able to do above all that you can ask or think. God wants you hot or cold, but hates the area of being unsure or undecided. It makes God sick to the stomach.

I had never really gotten religion, but that night, for the first time, I understood. I knew I did nothing wrong, yet no one would believe me. But whether they believe me or not, whether the judge keeps saying no or not, God is still God!

I cried for about an hour that Friday night, and the next Monday I went back to court. This time I wasn't afraid, not anxious, nor depressed. I believed that whether or not He saved me from my enemies; He Was Still Able! I rededicated my life that night at the Revival and that Monday, while waiting for court to begin, my attorney walked to me and said, "The case has been dismissed; all charges have been dropped, and you have been found and proven not guilty. The judge would like to speak to you."

He apologized for something that should have never come to court, "It will be erased from your records and please accept the court's apology."

I Have Served My God, Lord and Savior, ever since that Friday night, 37 years ago. I sing because I'm happy; I sing because I'm Free. His eye is on the sparrow and I know He watches me. There was a lesson I had to learn immediately, "No matter the trial, God Will See You Through. And even if He doesn't do it, He is Able and I Love Him Still."

Sis. Anonymous

CHAPTER 4

Who's Messing with My Mind?

The Invisible Rope

Many Psychologists have done tests to prove that people can be fooled to believe there is something stopping them from advancing further when, in reality, there is nothing there to stop them.

Hypothesis: People will trust in the behavior of others more than their own senses. (Top-down or Bottom-up processing)[2]

Bradley Norton

In 2010, there was a young man named Bradley Norton who came up with an idea to trick people into seeing things that were not really there. In reading this chapter, you will see how people refused to walk between Bradley and his appointed assistant as they kneeled down in a walkway as if they were holding a rope blocking the way. Adults as well as

---

[2] The Hypothesis Study, 2010 by: Bradley Norton, "The Invisible Rope Experiment"

the toddlers were seen walking behind the two gentlemen fearing that they would trip over an imaginary rope they were holding. In their minds, they saw a rope pulled and stretched across the walkway of the store.

In fear of falling down, all the customers in the store walked in another direction. Interestingly enough, in one case, a lady actually stumbled forward, because she was convinced that she got tangled up in the rope that the boys were pulling. As I watched these different tests being performed, over and over on different sets of people, I saw one man lift his foot up over the invisible rope as he walked by the boys reading his newspaper.

The most interesting one that I researched was these same two young men out in the country on a back road, one standing on each side of the street, leaning backwards with their hands in front of them, acting as if they were playing tug of war. One car drove up to the boys and stopped as if they were going to drive into the rope. Finally, after creeping closer and closer to the imaginary spot of the rope, the car slowly drove between the two boys. They performed this trap for hours, holding up traffic. It seems like someone would have gotten out of their car to ask what they were doing, but everyone waited until the boys let down this invisible rope.

Do you realize that this is how Satan and his little demonic followers play games with our minds? Every chance they get, they are scheming, plotting, and planning ways to trip us up, to hold us back, and to manipulate our progress by creating false pretenses of things that appear to be placed in front of you.

The Rope of Fear

One of the devil's most effective ropes used against mankind is the invisible rope of fear. Satan has created this certain type of trap by gathering and twisting a person's circumstances together, hoping that we would soon fall into his mental and spiritual traps. This is the rope that can cause you to lose focus on the real truth of a matter.

What was the point of the game that Mr. Bradley Norton played on so many people? Bradley proved to us in his experiment that if you allow people to control your thoughts, they can use anything or anyone to stop you from moving forward in your life. Maybe you're that person who feels you could never be tricked into a mental trap like that because you are too smart for that kind of elementary game. Well, my friend, Satan knows that his games of life can be very convincing without the leading and the guidance of Our Lord Jesus Christ!

If you are not led by the Holy Spirit into all truth, you are subject to being trapped, fooled, and deceived just like the next person in line. Remember dear friends, Satan was named, "The most cunning creature ever created." He has many tricks up his sleeve, and he sits crouched, waiting for his opportunity to capture you in your own lustful desires.

CHAPTER 5

The Chains that Challenged

My Change?

---

[28] And when he was come to the other side into the country of the Gergesenes, there met him two possessed with devils, coming out of the tombs, exceeding fierce, so that no man might pass by that way. [29] And, behold, they cried out, saying, what have we to do with thee, Jesus, thou Son of God? art thou come hither to torment us before the time?

Matthew 8:28 -29 KJV

[1] And they came over unto the other side of the sea, into the country of the Gadarenes. [2] And when he was come out of the ship, immediately there, met him out of the tombs a man with an unclean spirit, [3] Who had [his] dwelling among the tombs; and no man could bind him, no, not with chains: [4] Because that he had been often bound with fetters and chains, and the chains had been plucked asunder by him, and the fetters broken in pieces: neither could any [man] tame him. [5] And always, night and day, he was in the mountains, and in the tombs, crying, and cutting himself with stones.

Mark 5:1-5 KJV

²⁶ And they arrived at the country of the Gadarenes, which is over against Galilee. ²⁷ And when he went forth to land, there met him out of the city a certain man, which had devils long time, and ware no clothes, neither abode in [any] house, but in the tombs. ²⁸ When he saw Jesus, he cried out, and fell down before him, and with a loud voice said, what have I to do with thee, Jesus, [thou] Son of God most high? I beseech thee, torment me not. ²⁹ (For he had commanded the unclean spirit to come out of the man. For oftentimes it had caught him: and he was kept bound with chains and in fetters; and he broke the bands, and was driven of the devil into the wilderness.) ³⁰ And Jesus asked him, saying, what is thy name? And he said, Legion: because many devils were entered into him.

Luke 8:26-30 KJV

In the three accounts given in the story of *The Demon Possessed Man of Gergesenes*, we see a very grim scene unfold with a man who has, not just one but legions, thousands of evil spirits at work in his life. While it gives us no insight into how he came to be in this state, the outcome is plain; he is a tormented soul, not given rest day or night. He is so distraught by his condition and the unrelenting torture of his soul that he cuts himself on stones, goes around day and night crying out, and becomes a physical danger to those around him.

A psychiatrist would no doubt label this man as a paranoid schizophrenic; someone whose psyche has been shattered and driven by irrational fears, becoming dangerous to himself and others.

The modern reader is in no doubt horrified to read how people attempted to chain this man, but their attempts were, in actuality, attempts of mercy to keep him from further harming himself or others. They could have simply killed him, but they recognized there was something at work in him that was making him behave as he did.

Powerless to do anything else, they attempt to secure him to at least keep him safe; however, even that kindness had denied him. The demons enable him to tear away the physical fetters that might have helped ease him, but refuse to release him from the spiritual bonds. In the end, we see this man forced by the spirits to dwell in the tombs, a little more than dead himself.

Then, one day, a Man steps onto the shore from a small

fishing boat. Driven by the spirits, the demon possessed man runs to this Man and falls at His feet. The spirits recognize who Jesus is, but the man, himself, probably had no idea. Nevertheless, he is freed when Jesus casts the spirits out into a herd of swine. Mark numbers them at about 2000, which were on a nearby cliff.

Can you imagine what day-to-day life was like for this man? One moment, his mind is chaotic and fragmented, hearing voices, some threatening him and others telling him to hurt himself or others. And in another moment, he sees horrible images that no one else can see, played over and over before him. He is powerless to stop them, even in his sleep. He cuts himself with stones, maybe as an effort to try and deal with the emotional pain or possibly due to hallucinations. The wounds were untreated, unwashed, and would fester, becoming severely infected. His body is wrecked and his whole perception of reality is called into question every minute of every day until suddenly there is peace.

The voices stop. The images cease. All he sees is a Man standing by the sea. He hears the breeze, the seabirds, the lapping of small waves on the shore, and the voices of other men on the boat. He realizes the condition of his clothes and his body; perhaps he feels embarrassed. But Jesus and the disciples soon have him washed, dressed, and his wounds healed.

When the swine keepers bring back the people of the city to the seaside, the people see the man who has been the terror of the countryside, sitting calmly, clean, and clothed at the feet of Jesus. They knew from the account of the swine herders, and now from the account of their own eyes, something beyond amazing has occurred. They knew the power of the spirits that held this man. They had seen him break iron bonds, breaking free from the men who tried to restrain him. And yet, all it took was one word from this Man, and all that power fled. The people's reaction was Fear. They begged Jesus to depart, and He did so after instructing the man to remain and show himself to his friends and family, telling them of how God delivered him.

Mercifully, few of us can say that we have lived as tormented and terrible a life as this man. However, we all experience emotional and physical pain at some point in our life. While it may not be directly demonically induced, we know that the enemies of our souls are forever watchful for ways to trap and ensnare us. Many of us know that we have brought hurt

61

to our lives, but God is not hampered by the manner in which the hurts occurred.

We can fail to receive healing and deliverance when we try to accomplish it on our own or by our own means. Look closer at the story of this man. He obviously had friends and family, because Jesus instructs him to show himself to them. Without doubt, these people loved and cared for him, but were completely helpless to stop his descent into madness. With all the wisdom of that age, they somehow found a way to restrain him, so that he might at least be kept like an animal, chained, but safe. As the demons that infested him were not willing to allow him to remain as so, he is driven from the very ones who cared for him and may have been able to otherwise help him.

How many times have you reached out to a family member or friend who was hurting, and your efforts to help failed? How many times have others reached out to you, and what they offered was not enough to free you?

Our freedom can only come when we truly surrender to our Lord; when we come to Him truthfully and openly, revealing our condition to Him, and allowing Him to remove the chains, the hurts, and the shame that bind us. The same Savior, who with a word delivered this demon possessed man, can and will with a word heal and deliver you when you come to Him.

CHAPTER 6

Locked in Lodabar

Here's a story about the young grandchild of King Saul, Mephibosheth, in 2 Samuel 4:4; Samuel tells the story as follows:

There was a time in Israel, after David became king, where the family's nurse of Saul house tried to save Mephibosheth from danger, but her loving help for the child was not enough to set him free from his fears, which were imbedded in him by his nurse and rumor in the city.

David became king after Saul and Jonathan were killed in battle. Mephibosheth allowed the fear of dying at the hands of King David to trap him in an unprofitable land called Lodabar. Mephibosheth lived in the house of Machir, located in Lodabar; where he unknowingly hid from prosperity, growth, and deliverance because the citizens of Israel told him that his handicap would be the reason for him being killed instead of being promoted.

Rumors and lies can and will keep you bound if you allow them to create realities in your mind. The rumor was that there was a decree set out by the king for all who had any handicap or physical disability to be done away with. This decree happens to be one of the reasons this boy's nurse picked him up, thinking she was saving him, and ran in the opposite direction of the king's palace and his soldiers.

It is such an alarming situation when people are not aware of the call and blessings spoken over your life. Their assistance to you can be more of a liability than an asset.

The child's nurse thought she was truly helping him by hiding him. She did not realize the promise that King David had made with his best friend Jonathan. Before Jonathan died, he had a heartfelt discussion with David, asking David not to kill his children when he became king of Israel. It was customary for the new king to get rid of or dispose of all people, staff, leaders, soldiers, and family members who were part of the previous king's cabinet. David agreed to bless Jonathan's seed when the time came for him to take over as Israel's new king.

What part does Mephibosheth play in being tricked or

trapped? Well, it's easy; this young boy spent years hiding from his blessings until a close friend of his, by the name of Ziba, came and spoke life into his dead situation. Ziba knew just where Mephibosheth was hiding. He knew Mephibosheth was trapped, broken, afraid, and disconnected with the king, because he too had been there before. So, he took it upon himself to show his friend a way out of this unprofitable house in Lodabar.

The story tells us that David comes before the king, still bound in his mind, and begins to question the king, "Why would you save a dead dog like me?"

I would imagine King David saying to himself, "Yes, he has been bound too long. He doesn't even think of himself as a worthy candidate for the king's table and palace."

Later, Ziba becomes jealous of Mephibosheth's new lease on life and tries to use his weakness against him by lying to King David about Mephibosheth's integrity. Sometimes the same people who are there to assist you in getting out of a situation soon become your greatest challenge in staying out. They can become your most ruthless enemy, and the key to your demise. It's been proven time and time again that people change their opinions about you when they see you coming out of bondage and prospering more than they are. Most people will claim they desire to see you free from the chains of life; however, at the same time, those claims are based on what that individual will get out of the deal.

My friends, pay close attention to those around you and their motives when they ask to help you up or out of Lodabar. This story is so interesting to me, because it allows us to view the mindset of the individuals who will make room for us to stay in the same old rut, year after year.

CHAPTER 7

The Pitiful Pool Party

---

[1] After this there was a feast of the Jews, and Jesus went up to Jerusalem. [2] Now there is in Jerusalem by the Sheep Gate a pool, which is called in Hebrew, Bethesda, having five porches. [3] In these lay a great multitude of sick people, blind, lame, paralyzed, waiting for the moving of the water. [4] For an angel went down at a certain time into the pool and stirred up the water; then whoever stepped in first, after the stirring of the water, was made well of whatever disease he had. [5] Now a certain man was there who had an infirmity thirty-eight years. [6] When Jesus saw him lying there, and knew that he already had been in that condition a long time, He said to him, "Do you want to be made well?"

[7] The sick man answered Him, "Sir, I have no man to put me into the pool when the water is stirred up; but while I am coming, another steps down before me."

[8] Jesus said to him, "Rise, take up your bed and walk." [9] And immediately the man was made well, took up his bed, and

walked.

And that day was the Sabbath. [10] The Jews therefore said to him who was cured, "It is the Sabbath; it is not lawful for you to carry your bed."

[11] He answered them, "He who made me well said to me, 'Take up your bed and walk.'"

[12] Then they asked him, "Who is the Man who said to you, 'Take up your bed and walk'?" [13] But the one who was healed did not know who it was, for Jesus had withdrawn, a multitude being in that place. [14] Afterward Jesus found him in the temple, and said to him, "See, you have been made well. Sin no more, lest a worse thing come upon you."

[15] The man departed and told the Jews that it was Jesus who had made him well.

John 5:1-15

Ever been to a pool party where everyone is dressed in their swimsuit, but no one is getting in the pool? Cousins, friends, and long-lost family members are all standing around in the hot sun complaining about how hot it is, but no one is getting in the water to cool off. Common sense would tell you that if you are invited to a pool party, and no one is getting in, something is wrong with this party.

You look around and the pool is clean; the water looks inviting; the ladies look nice in their swimsuits, and the homies are in their shorts and muscle shirts, but it has been hours and still no water has slashed outside of the pool, because no one has jumped in. Why would we call it a pool party? Is it only because the house has a pool there? Or were you expected to get in when you changed into your swimwear? This happens at every pool party you go to, even at the beach.

We become hostages to the thoughts of other party goers who are just standing around looking and waiting for someone else to make the first move and jump in. Yes, it's a pitiful situation when you don't move due to those around you, because they have chosen not to move and stand still.

I would like to share the mindset of the man in the above passage who John, one of Jesus' disciples, described as laying at the Pool of Bethesda on one of the 5 porches of infirmity. Research has proven that an infirmity is not the actual disease; it is the symptom of a disease trying to take over the mind, body, and soul.

Jesus explains that he walks up to one of these five porches where this man laid, and asks him, "Why lay you here for 38 years, leaning on the edge of the pool?"

The man replied, "Every time I get ready to get in, someone jumps in before me and I end up missing out on my healing once again."

It was interesting that Jesus asked the man this question, because the rumor was that at the time the angel came and troubled the waters, the first to jump in was the one to be healed and delivered from their ailments. How can a person choose to live for 38 years right on the edge of the pool watching, time after time, as the angel troubled the water, and not just roll over into the pool? This is the mentality of a great amount of people in this world. We watch as others are blessed, and instead of making something happen, we complain, hoping something will one day happen to us.

The Blame Game

Every time I get ready to get in; someone else gets in before me; no one will help me get in; I tried, but no one would show me how to do it; I really want to, but that's for someone else to do.

These are just a few of the excuses people come up with to justify their laziness, sluggard attitude and their reason for not progressing.

Excuses

He that is good for making excuses is seldom good for anything else.

Benjamin Franklin

Mr. Franklin was correct in making this statement, because very few people make excuses for everything they mess up on. You can ask yourself the question: why do they make so many excuses all day long? Is it due to them being afraid of the true reason why they did not accomplish a certain thing in the beginning?

Take me, for instance. When I was in middle school, I got to a point where I chose to act crazy and unconcerned about life when it came to my schoolwork, homework, and house chores. I had decided to become stagnant and lazy, but in doing so my scores on my test dropped, my will to do and accomplish awards dropped, and the relationship with my friend started to falter, until one day; my best friend said, "We may not be friends after I say this, but you need to stop blaming everyone else for your faults and failures in school, church, and in life."

I remember him telling me to grow up, and that if I did something wrong, I should take the blame for it. That was probably the hardest thing I had ever heard in that time of my life, but it was one of the eye openers for me to change my ways. I was good at passing the buck on to the next person for me not passing my test—sound familiar?

"The teacher should have taught that part of the subject better." It almost sounds like Mary and Martha in the bible when they said to Jesus, "If you were here, he would not have died," speaking of their brother Lazarus. Or what about Adam, "Lord, it was that woman YOU gave me who tricked me into eating the forbidden fruit."

Man is good at making excuses for not doing right. The man at the pool was more pitiful than the rest, because at least they got in the water before him, which shows that they probably got tired of sitting around a pool full of negativity, lies, and crybabies. There will come a time in your life when you will say to yourself, when am I going to change my focus, and look toward Jesus for my healing and deliverance, and turn from people who are not going anywhere?

Imprisonment to Excuses

Change does not roll in on the wheels of inevitability but comes through continuous struggle. And so, we must straighten our backs and work for our freedom. A man can't ride you unless your back is bent. [3]

Martin Luther King, Jr

What will it take for us to move on and upward to a more respectable lifestyle? It takes courage to move beyond the confines of unmovable people. Jesus has a very interesting way of showing us that our next move is based on our next thought or how we follow the next instruction given to us.

---

[3] The Death of Evil upon the Seashore,' sermon given at the Cathedral of St. John the Divine, New York City, 17 May 1956

Jesus tells the man, speaking with all authority, to pick up his bed and walk.

What is your bed, what is that bed called that's holding you down and convincing you rest and relax as life goes on?

I could imagine the people around the pool as Jesus gives this direct command on this sacred Jewish Sabbath Day, in which the law says no man is supposed to work. Jesus knew it was time for the man to decide if he would live there in that same place another year or break the Sabbath law.

When your deliverance is right in your face, you would be foolish to ignore your help. There was once a story told about a man who God promised to send him help. As he was waiting for God, a storm came and overtook the man. As he sat treading in the water, God sent three different individuals to save him, but he turned them all down, looking for God to come some other way to save him.

When your focus is on God moving in the way you expect him to move, you may miss out on the blessings that are waiting there for you. The lifeguard was there in a boat, another came in a helicopter, and another with a rope, but he refused all of them three times over.

The poor man at the pool of Bethesda would have rather faced death and destruction than accept help from a stranger who had the ability to do more than put him in a pool of water; this stranger had the ability to speak to his spirit and say get up and get out.

It is important to remember, the mind is a terrible thing to waste, and the mind is wasted when you don't have Jesus inside guiding and instructing your next move.

CHAPTER 8

When Love Won't Let You Leave

A Salty Situation

But Lot's wife looked back as she was following behind him, and she turned into a pillar of salt.

Genesis 19:26

How many times have you heard the phrase, "But he (or she) really loves me?" On most occasions, this phrase is used in some type of negative scenario, such as a close friend or family member's domestic case of violence.

"Girl! Wake up, I don't understand why you don't hurry up and pack your children's clothes along with your things and come move with me? Or better yet, go get your own place so you can have some peace of mind."

Sadly, these types of conversations are discussed every minute of the day with the people we love.

I'm reminded of a time my sister was opening a can as she

was cooking. She only cut ¾ of the can's lid because she was not focusing on anything besides getting her dinner ready for her family. Since the lid was not fully cut away, she could not get all the food out of the can. It was then that she pushed the lid down to open the can wider.

What a mess that was. She started screaming for help because two of her fingers were caught in the can, with the razor-sharp lid against her fingertips. As bad as she wanted to get her fingers out of this can, without cutting them off, she had to stop and let someone else figure out the safest way to help her get free. This would not be a fast pace, snatch your fingers out move. This was going to take some strategic planning.

After a few minutes of bending the can, slightly shifting her fingers, a gap appeared between the lid and the body of the can that allowed her to slip her fingers out. Her eyes, which were full of fear, were now full of celebrative tears. How happy she was that she was out of that mess!

Well, life situations can be just that devastating and more.

Sodom and Gomorrah

When we read the story about Sodom and Gomorrah, most people focus their attention on the homosexual attempts on the two Angelic Men who were sent to pronounce judgment on that city. But there is far more going on in this story besides the desire to be intimate with these men. The main focus of this story could be that Lot's wife *was turned* into a pillar of salt, but that is not it. I believe the focal point of this passage of scripture should be *Why!* was Lot's wife turned into that pillar of salt?

When we read the story, we already know and see that they were told not to look back after they finally decided to leave Sodom by the force of the Angels. Time of judgment had arisen, and now things were about to become catastrophic in Sodom and Gomorrah. God's judgment was now being pronounced on the sin and the ways that the people had adopted.

If you would go back and read the story a bit more in detail, you will see that the angels had suggested that Lot and his family pack up and decide to move out of the wicked city. But when the approach, the attempt, or the attack on angels became very aggressive, Lot and his family were forced to leave immediately.

Genesis Chapter 18
Abraham Has A Visitation from God

In chapter 18 of Genesis, God sends angels to visit Abraham and to discuss the judgment that is about to be placed on Sodom and Gomorrah. The Lord tells Abraham that He is going to pronounce judgment on Sodom because of the wickedness and the level that it had reached in the eyes of God.

You will remember that Abraham begins to negotiate with God on saving that city, because his nephew, by the name of Lot, along with Lot's family, are citizens of Sodom. Abraham then says to God while they're talking, "If I could find at least 50 righteous people in Sodom, God, will you spare the city?"

And God replies to Abraham by saying yes! I can imagine Abraham's saying, *wow, that was easier than I thought*; so he goes on to ask God if he was to find 45 righteous people in Sodom, would God spare the land? God replies to Abraham the second time and tells him yes, "I will spare the land if you found 45 righteous people."

Abraham continues his negotiation with God by increments of five and ten until he gets down to asking God the last question. "God! If I find just 10 righteous people living in Sodom and Gomorrah, Will You Still spare the city from destruction?"

And God says to him for the last time, "If you find 10 righteous people in that city, I will then spare the land."

Interestingly enough, that's how chapter 18 ends, with negotiating from 50 people who are righteous down to 10.

The Two Angels Appear in Sodom and Gomorrah to Pronounce Destruction

"And there came two angels to Sodom at even; and Lot sat in the gate of Sodom: and Lot seeing them rose up to meet them; and he bowed himself with his face toward the ground."

Genesis 19:1

So now here we are in chapter 19 of Genesis. If you would remember chapter 18 left off saying that God would spare the land and would not pronounce destruction on Sodom and Gomorrah if He found ten righteous people. But if we look into the scripture and look closer at the text that is written before us, we will see these two angels going to Sodom and Gomorrah to pronounce destruction or to destroy the city.

This implies that between the end of chapter 18 of Genesis and the beginning of chapter 19, Abraham did not find ten righteous people in the entire city. What a sad commentary, to be living in a city where there are not 10 people who have committed or dedicated their lives to the true and living God.

A Bad Business Deal

If we were to look closer at verse number one in Genesis 19, we would see that the two angels approached Sodom and Gomorrah and they met up with Lot, who was sitting at the entrance of the gate. For those who understand customs and manners in the Jewish lifestyle, you would understand that it was there at the entrance of the gate is where all the business-minded people sat and did business; it was there at the entrance of the gate where deals were made; it was at the entrance of the gate where negotiations and satisfactions of debts were sealed. So here we are with two angels sent from God to destroy a city, and the nephew of Abraham sitting at the entrance point of this city that is about to go down.

Verse 1 — It's funny because Lot recognizes the angels immediately. The Bible says he bows his face down to the ground in honor of their heavenly glow. Anytime there's a visitation from God in the bible, you see that the first thing the person does is bow down before the Holiness of God. It has nothing to do with the individual themselves; it has all to do with the glory of God that is upon or within that person. We all know that the person we bow down to as King of kings and Lord of lords is our Lord and Savior Jesus, the Christ, but it is here that the glory of God is seen at the entrance of the gate by Lot himself. It is my exegetical thought that Lot knew sooner or later God was going to show up and pronounce judgment upon that city.

How could one live in a city where there's so much wickedness, and God does not rectify the problem? I can imagine these men telling Lot that they are about to destroy this city in a few days and it's time for him to make up his mind where they're going to move to next.

What we have to remember is, when God gets ready to take care of business, it does not matter how we feel, what we think, or what we say. However, God will take into consideration our thoughts as He did with Abraham, but if there is not a change, when it's all said and done, God will follow through on His first thought.

For we read in **Romans 6:23, "That the wages of sin is death and the gift of God is eternal life..."** what we must understand is it's up to us what happens in our lives, when it comes to God's will being manifested fully. God, In His Love and Sovereignty, still put Adam and Eve on the outside of the Garden of Eden, for the sin and disobedience that was committed. Not only did God evict them from the garden, but He also put angels at the entrance of the garden to keep Adam and his wife out. When God establishes a law, He expects it to be followed with willful obedience.

Lot knew that the disobedience and sinful nature of the men of Sodom would be practiced on the two men from God, so Lot tried to help the situation.

Verse 2 — "And he said, Behold now, my lords, turn in, I

pray you, into your servant's house, and tarry all night, and wash your feet, and ye shall rise up early, and go on your ways. And they said, Nay; but we will abide in the street all night."

Lot invites the heavenly angels to come and stay in his house for the night. He offers to wash their feet; he welcomes them in to clean themselves up. Lot knew their coming was about business, so he encouraged them to leave first thing in the morning to carry out their appointed assignment.

It was customary for the host of a house to wash the feet of his visitors and to prepare a great meal for them. Remember, Jesus had a problem with His disciples and the scribes when Mary washed His feet with her hair. Jesus said, "No one in this house has done nothing to welcome me since I've walked in here. But this woman has not stopped rubbing my feet (or washing my feet)." So, Lot was following what we would call good ole hospitality morals.

Verse 3 — "And he pressed upon them greatly; and they turned in unto him, and entered into his house; and he made them a feast, and did bake unleavened bread, and they did eat."

Not one true man or woman of God wants to see another child of God hurt or injured in ministry. When a person steps out to do God's will, it is a unified effort amongst all the believers to see this task completed. So, whether it's me doing the job, or you, it is the responsibility of our brothers and sisters to cover us in prayer, to encourage each other during hard times, and to pick each other up when we fall short.

After Lot pressed it upon them to stay, the angels replied to Lot, "No thank you, we will sleep in the center of the courtyard (the square of the city)." Lot then persuades them that this is not a safe thing to do, so he convinces them to stay in his house. Once the two angels agree to stay in Lot's house, the Bible tells us that Lot goes in and prepares a meal for these men, and they eat unleavened bread.

Verse 4 — "But before they lay down, the men of the city, even the men of Sodom, compassed the house round, both old and young, all the people from every quarter."

Someone is probably asking, "What does all of this have to do with Lots' wife being turned into a pillar of salt?"

I'm glad you asked, but let me bring out all the details to

satisfy the facts about Lot's wife.

We see here that before these two men lay down to go to sleep, everyone in the city has a circumference of the house of Lot. All the men of the city are now in a tactical position to overtake Lots' house. This goes to show us that there is always somebody watching your house, watching what you do in ministry, listening closely to what you say. Think about it. Someone had to share the news in the city about these visitors. Someone had to start the rumors that these two strange men were in Lot's house.

Imagine, or envision, all the spectators who were there. They were closely looking to see what was going to happen next at Pastor Lot's Church, or his house. These two men were not afraid of the crowd. They were not persuaded, at any point, to run from the crowd. The only thing on their minds was to get those of righteousness out before the judgment fell on the ungodly.

Verse 5 — "And they called unto Lot, and said unto him, where are the men which came into thee this night? Bring them out unto us, that we may know them."

I can picture Lot bouncing off the walls because he knew the intentions of the sinful men. The same as his uncle, Abraham; negotiating with God to spare the lives in Sodom is the same way Lot was praying and negotiating for the lives of those two strangers. But the men of the city do not want anything from Lot.

"And Lot went out at the door unto them, and shut the door after him, and said, I pray you, brethren, do not so wickedly. Behold now, I have two daughters which have not known man; let me, I pray you, bring them out unto you, and do ye to them as is good in your eyes: only unto these men do nothing; for therefore came they under the shadow of my roof. And they said, Stand back.

And they said again, this one fellow came in to sojourn, and he will need to be a judge: now will we deal worse with thee, than with them. And they pressed sore upon the man, even Lot, and came near to break the door. But the men put forth their hand, and pulled Lot into the house to them, and shut to the door.

And they smote the men that were at the door of the house with blindness, both small and great: so that they wearied themselves to find the door. And the men said unto Lot, Hast thou here any besides? Son in law, and thy sons, and thy daughters, and whatsoever thou hast in the city, bring them

out of this place: For we will destroy this place, because the cry of them is waxen great before the face of the LORD; and the LORD hath sent us to destroy it. And Lot went out, and spake unto his sons in law, which married his daughters, and said, Up, get you out of this place; for the LORD will destroy this city. But he seemed as one that mocked unto his sons in law.

And when the morning arose, then the angels hastened Lot, saying, Arise, take thy wife, and thy two daughters, which are here; lest thou be consumed in the iniquity of the city. And while he lingered, the men laid hold upon his hand, and upon the hand of his wife, and upon the hand of his two daughters; the LORD being merciful unto him: and they brought him forth, and set him without the city, and it came to pass, when they had brought them forth abroad, that he said, Escape for thy life; look not behind thee, neither stay thou in all the plain; escape to the mountain, lest thou be consumed, and Lot said unto them, Oh, not so, my Lord: Behold now, thy servant hath found grace in thy sight, and thou hast magnified thy mercy, which thou hast shewed unto me in saving my life; and I cannot escape to the mountain, lest some evil take me, and I die: Behold now, this city is near to flee unto, and it is a little one: Oh, let me escape thither, (is it not a little one?) and my soul shall live.

And he said unto him, See, I have accepted thee concerning this thing also, that I will not overthrow this city, for the which thou hast spoken. Haste thee, escape thither; for I cannot do any thing till thou be come thither. Therefore the name of the city was called Zoar.

The sun was risen upon the earth when Lot entered into Zoar. Then the LORD rained upon Sodom and upon Gomorrah brimstone and fire from the LORD out of heaven; and he overthrew those cities, and all the plain, and all the inhabitants of the cities, and that which grew upon the ground. But his wife looked back from behind him, and she became a pillar of salt and Abraham gat up early in the morning to the place where he stood before the LORD: And he looked toward Sodom and Gomorrah, and toward all the land of the plain, and beheld, and, lo, the smoke of the country went up as the smoke of a furnace.

Wait a minute! Hold up! If all this chaos is going on, with the men of the city banging at the doors and windows, the two angels are now in a defensive mode, and Lot is being told he and his family have to leave the city right now and NOT TO LOOK BACK! — Then maybe you are thinking like me—what in the world would persuade Lot's wife to look back?

Lustful Look Back

"But every man is tempted, when he is drawn away of his own lust, and enticed."

James 1:14

In Judaism, one common view of Lot's wife turning to salt was as punishment for disobeying the angels' warning. By looking back at the "evil cities," she betrayed her secret longing for that way of life. She was deemed unworthy to be saved and, thus, was turned to a pillar of salt. There are many people who harbor secret longing for people, places, and things. It is here where the commentary of theologians have figured that her longing for the ways of Sodom and Gomorrah caused her to become stiff, rigid, and immobile.

Have you ever been in a situation where you wanted to move further in life, but nothing you wanted seemed to be in front of you? It seems like everything you thought you were going to need was left behind you. This could very well be the reason Lot's wife was disobedient and turned back.

Another commentary expresses a different viewpoint of Jewish beliefs that says Lot's wife was turned into a pillar of salt because Lot requested salt from his wife to be offered to the two traveling angels. His wife told Lot it was a bad custom to offer the salt from their household, so she went house to house looking for salt in the neighborhood and informed the men of the houses about the two travelers.

This idea is not expressed in the Bible, only in Jewish teachings. Others believe her actions suggest she identified with the people of Sodom. Her failure to flee God's punishment becomes a vivid warning to others in life. Strangely, some commentators believe she was looking back to see if her daughters were following behind or if her father's house was surviving the wrath.

There are so many ways to look at the reasons why she turned back. Let's take a closer look from my viewpoint on some of the options she had, and choices she made. When reading the story about Lot's wife and how she looked back, remember it gave the impression that she had a secret connection, or a spiritual tie, to Sodom and Gomorrah.

Losing Look Back

"No temptation has overtaken you that is not common to man. God is faithful, and he will not let you be tempted beyond your

ability, but with the temptation he will also provide the way of escape, that you may be able to endure it."

1 Corinthians 10:13

The Bible very plainly tells us that God will always make a way of escape for his children. He will never allow the devil to trap you or to leave you hostage in a place where God cannot reach you. We must be willing and eager to move when God tells us to move. If the Lord says He will make a way of escape out of every situation, then Lot and his family should have made it out scot-free.

But it is Lot's wife who brought questions to the will and the ways of God. Could it be the fact that she had a lustful love for the ways of the city? If we would really be transparent with ourselves, and be real with our feelings on the inside of us, we too have procrastinated on moving forward and leaving people behind, because of our own lustful love for the situations we have been in.

This is why some people cannot leave domestic violence situations, nor can they walk away from being abused physically, psychologically, emotionally, or spiritually. Have you ever seen a person who was so miserable in a situation they're in, but they stay there anyway because of their lustful love of attention?

I used to know some people who stayed with their spouse just to have negative attention, just to be noticed, just to have five or ten minutes of their time, whether it was positive or abusive, they just wanted the attention.

It's like a couple, whether married or not, who are constantly breaking up, but use the children to keep bringing them back in a negative situation. This has nothing to do with love; so, it must be lust.

I believe that Lot's wife expressed some type of lustful love when she looked back at a city that was full of sin, shame, and sexual stability.

Last Look Back

"Jesus answered him, "If anyone loves me, he will keep my word, and my Father will love him, and we will come to him and make our home with him. 24 Whoever does not love me does not keep my words. And the word that you hear is not mine, but the Father who sent me. 25 "These things I have

spoken to you while I am still with you. [26] But the Helper, the Holy Spirit, whom the Father will send in my name, he will teach you all things and bring to your remembrance all that I have said to you.

[27] Peace I leave with you; my peace I give to you. Not as the world gives do I give to you. Let not your hearts be troubled, neither let them be afraid. [28] You heard me say to you, 'I am going away, and I will come to you.' If you loved me, you would have rejoiced, because I am going to the Father, for the Father is greater than I.

[29] And now I have told you before it takes place, so that when it does take place you may believe. [30] I will no longer talk much with you, for the ruler of this world is coming. He has no claim on me, [31] but I do as the Father has commanded me, so that the world may know that I love the Father. Rise, let us go from here."

St. John 14:23-31

Could it possibly be that Lot's wife looks back because she felt like she would be lost without her familiar surroundings? Maybe she forgot the scripture tells us that God will never leave us, nor will He forsake us; He will be with us even until the end of the world.

When we forget the goodness of God in the land of the living and forget that God is the one who created us and gave breath to our bodies, we put ourselves in a predicament where we can be found lost.

No one really likes to be lost. One of the most frustrating things in the world is to ride in the car with a person who is lost and refuse to ask for help from someone who can get us out of that situation.

Ever been driving by yourself to a city you've never been to before? The roads are dark; the people are unkind; the city shuts down early, and you have no sense of idea how close you are to your destination. The first thing one would want to do is to turn around and go back to what they call home. For you, who are Bible readers, you will remember when Moses was leading the People out of Egypt; the Lord told Moses to tell them that He was going to take them the long way around. The reason God was taking the Israelites the long way around was because He said if He took them the short way, it would be easy for them to turn back to where He had just brought them out of.

Sometimes God will allow you to go through things and

situations, be put in frustrating trials, tribulations, tests, and the traumas that are full of tension. But He does it to let you know you will never, ever, have to feel lost, because He is there with you.

Whenever I have felt loss when traveling from one place to another, when traveling from one state to another state that I was unfamiliar with, I become nervous, paranoid, almost schizophrenic, and I lack trust in my own senses. Why! Because I'm in an area that I'm not familiar with. This very well could be one of the reasons why Lot's wife looked back, because she was going to an area that she was not familiar with.

Lonely Look Back

"Then the LORD God said, "It is not good that the man should be alone; I will make him a helper fit for him."

Genesis 2:18

Think about it, she had been living in Sodom and Gomorrah all those years. All of her friends were there. It was the place where they had considered it to be their retirement home, but now, Lot and his family's living status was interrupted by God because of sin. How do you just walk away from something you've had for years? How did you just pack your bags and move forward and never look back to see what you're leaving? There is something in your psyche or spirit that urges you to take that last look. As we can see today, that last look back can be your *last look* ever.

"Keep your life free from love of money, and be content with what you have, for he has said, I will never leave you nor forsake you."

Hebrews 13:5

Walking away from things that you are used to is not an easy task when it's you making the decision. You really have to think about the big picture before you make that move. However, when God is the one orchestrating the move, you don't have time to think about it. All you have time to do is move when God tells you to move, and trust that everything is going to be alright.

Yes, I know, easier said than done! But the Bible says, "Trust in the Lord with all your heart, and lean not to your own understanding, in all your ways acknowledge Him, and He will direct our path."

That's even in this scenario or story, as with Lot and his family. Somebody did not trust God with all their heart. Can you guess who that somebody was?

RESOLVED: Could that person be you, who's struggling with making decisions that will change your whole life? I'm here today to tell you that if you would give God your undivided attention, and if you would lean your ear towards His mouth, He will speak clearly to your heart.

Don't allow situations, people, places, or possessions to be the reason you become stagnated. The Lord said He will never leave us, nor ever forsake us. Sometimes it's hard for us to make the right move, because we are waiting for people to give us the okay, or to certify our decisions. But if you are going to follow after God, the Bible said no man can say he wants to follow God and turn back from the plow.

Once you say you're going to follow God, and once you say He is your leader, your guy, your direction in the time of storms, your protection when the wind blows, your strong tower in the time of trouble; If He is your bridge over troubled waters, then Trust Him, even when you can't trace

Him.

PRAYER: Dear God, I pray for each and every person who reads this chapter, and each and every person who is struggling with a situation in their life.

Father, I pray you would move upon them like never before. Lord, I pray you will wrap your loving arms around them and give them the strength to walk away from things that are causing them to be separate from your will, your ways, and your worship. Lord, let them know it is okay to be obedient to your voice, for you said in your word that my sheep know my voice, and the stranger they will not follow.

Lord, keep us come in your perfect will and give us strength to face every situation that causes us to procrastinate in Your Kingdom. Amen!

CHAPTER 9

It's A Personal Problem

"Many refuse to exercise the gifts God has given them to preach, teach, to lead a congregation in prayer, or sing, because they do not feel worthy."

Don Fortner

Solitary Confinement

But Lot's wife looked back as she was following behind him, and she turned into a pillar of salt.

Genesis 19:26

How many people do you know who are struggling with personal issues that they don't want anyone to know about?

They spend night after night dealing with personal demons that will not give them any rest. Whether it is depression, anger, or sadness, they seem to be losing the battles of life, as they sit in solitary thinking about every failing moment that has gone wrong in their lives. Let's take a closer look at a personal testimony from an individual who went through some things in life in which they thought they would never come out of.

Could you imagine being in a world that appears to be dark everywhere you go? Walking around in the light, but unable to recognize the light that is there? Listen to this testimony of a girl who was tricked by her boyfriend who lured her into prostitution as they went to house parties, which became private parties, where he just dropped her off and said he would be back.

Testimony of being Tricked and Trapped

Hello, my name is *******; I want you to pay very close attention to my story. I pray that as you read my story, you would allow it to minister to the situation you may be going through openly or in secret.

I've been subjected to mind games all my life. Early on, my father would play mind games or implant subliminal seeds of low self-esteem into me. If I made a bad decision in school, my father would often ask me to make a choice to pick between being 'dumb' or 'stupid.' Whenever this man walked into the room, I was forced to stop what I was doing and acknowledge his presence. My father would simply walk into the room and say, "Alright... (and my name...)."

That was my que to say, "Hi dad," no matter how many times I may have already seen him around the house that same day.

It wasn't like he wasn't a loving father, but more like a tyrant who demanded to be worshipped. He would also allow me to witness him physically abusing my two older siblings. I dreaded getting older, as I knew that once I was big enough to be whipped, he was going to abuse me. If we were in public or around guests, he would make a spectacle out of me and my siblings by ordering around to fetch his beer, or other items, while my father and his guest (usually his brother) would watch us 'perform.' My father planted the seed early on that I was a debt to society, and I needed to pay back the universe (especially him) for being born.

When I was 3, an older female relative molested me.

This relative would often babysit me while my parents slept or were at work. At times, my relatives would be unusually cruel, inflicting fear on me by raising, yelling, or startling me. In a sense, she was like the predator in the Antwone Fisher movie; someone who enjoyed instilling fear of pain to keep her subject(s) submissive or quiet. Although she molested me just once (once too many), for ten years or so, I was absolutely terrified of her. She inherited a spirit that was similar to the one my father had in control of him.

As I became a woman, I attracted the same type of men. Men who were selfish, who spent, at times, more time in the mirror than I even have. One man in particular who I met in the club one night. We hooked up and talked for maybe about a month. On the phone one evening, this guy invited me to a bowling night that his homeboy was having.

"Just one thing...," he told me. "You have to dress extra sexy."

"What?" I said, confused. "To the bowling alley?"

"Yes," David replied. "Baby, you have to understand. If you are gonna want to be with me, then you gotta dress the part. I'm known for having beautiful women around me. So, you gotta show your t*ts and make sure your skirt is high. No pants! If you show up in pants, I'm sorry babe, but you gonna have to go back home."

I was numb and perplexed; yet this is what my new 'man' was asking from me, so I wanted to fulfill his request. I pulled up to the bowling alley, wearing a 't*tty top' and a mini skirt.

As I looked around, I noticed that everyone else, even the women, had on jeans and bowling shoes. I was the only one dressed like a prostitute. I felt so cheapened & humiliated. This man obviously didn't care enough. He didn't care that I was a bit chilly. He just wanted to violate me, then show what he pulled. David couldn't see the light in my eyes going dim. I kissed him *goodbye* that night, knowing in my heart I never wanted to see him again.

Years later, I went through mind games, even with my high school sweetheart.

Five years after high school, we ended up living together. Things were great in the beginning. He bought me flowers, told me repeatedly how much he loved me, he held my hand, etc., but then he would also begin to play mind games. He knew that I was absolutely petrified of his pet python.

You would think that normally a man who truly loved his woman would do everything he could to keep a distance between her and the snake. Yet he would often leave the phyton's cage half secure (despite my constant pleading). So, I would come home, and the 6' 5" snake would either be stretched out in the living room or standing straight up in the shower.

The 'I love yous' my man used to tell me, became, "Okay, I never really loved you."

Then when I confronted him about lying, his response was, "I didn't lie. When I said I was falling in love with you, I meant I was open to falling in love with you. It just didn't happen."

I yelled at him, "Stop playing these entrapping mind games with me! Acting like I'm crazy."

Even in my most recent relationship, I endured even more mind games. Although I try to practice being meek, if I *asked nicely* to get what I wanted, he would stigmatize me as being *passive aggressive*. Especially in arguments in which he was clearly wrong. For example, a case of him doing a *no call, no show*. He would withdraw himself, not answer his phone, listen to his voicemails, or read my text where I'm getting more and more upset with him. Allow me to throw in the towel and break up with him (as he knows it's a pet-peeve of mine to be ignored, I just think that's highly insensitive and disrespectful), then whenever we would break down & talk again, he would say, "See, you overreact when things get hard, how do I know I can trust you?"

Instead of being a real man, as the head, and coming to the negotiating table so we would work it out, he would access my leadership skills that I implemented during his emotional absence. He would allow me to be painted as uncommitted, although he passively aggressively orchestrated my failure. He knew that silence is not only golden, but it's power and he used his silence against me so he could blame me for overreacting and walking away all the time, knowing that the attention would be off of the subject at hand. The fact was that he was a *no call, no show* in the first place.

CHAPTER 10

Tasting a Tasteless Meal

When you sit to eat with a ruler, consider diligently what is before you...

Proverbs 23:1

Ivan Pavlov

In 1980, a Russian Physiologist stepped out and did an experiment on dogs which he called, 'Classical Conditioning.' In his testing, he wanted to find out the reasoning for dogs salivating when they see food, and if it would be possible to cause the dogs to salivate by hearing the sound of a bell and without food in front of them.

In the beginning, Pavlov started ringing a bell to see what reaction the dogs would have. In his testing, the dogs did not respond to the bell, in which he called 'Natural Stimulus.' But soon as they gave the dogs a bowl of food, the dogs began to salivate.

Pavlov took it upon himself to ring a bell as he put food in front of the dogs. After a while of ringing a bell, playing a metronome, and serving the food simultaneously, he soon stopped serving the food as the bells rang, and the salvation continued without the food being present. This proves the mind can play tricks on you when an unconditional response has been tampered with.

Pavlov called this reaction of the dog a 'Conditional Stimulus.' Leading to prove that as the dog thought he was seeing and tasting his food, as does man become tricked by others, making them react to things that are not visible to the eyes.

Proverbs 23:7 says, "Whatsoever a man thinketh in his heart, so is he." Take the child who has been called a dummy all of their life. On a daily basis, their parents have convinced them that they are dumb. They go to school thinking they are less fortunate than all the other children; so, when testing time comes, the child has already failed the test in their mind. When the teachers ask a question, the child slumps down, hiding in their seat because they don't believe they have the correct answer.

Could this all be due to the stereotypical acceptance that they are dumb? No one knows the sadness that a child endures within if you have never been in that situation. All you can do is imagine, but can never have a true understanding of the pain. I was one of those children who was called ignorant, dumb, stupid, and sorry at times; all because I messed up on a test or a classroom assignment. I knew it was because my mother expected the best out of her children, and out of anger, she said certain things.

Unlike some of the others I knew, I made myself push harder to be appreciated and smiled at. I looked forward to that day when I could hear my mother say, "Good job; great effort; excellent try!" or even "That's better than the last time."

Those small little words can make or break a person's character. Anyone can be cruel; children can be very cruel to each other, even in sports or the classroom. Some students become losers due to the peer pressure they face on campus. Children never want to do anything wrong in front of another child. They have to be at their best, because when Mr. or Mrs. Teacher calls out your test score in class, it determines the outcome of their day.

Could you imagine being called stupid? Not just by your parents, but by everyone who walks past you at school? What about walking around the school with a dunce or dummy sign posted to your back by some evil classmate? This could drive a person into insanity. Hearing dummy at home, at school, and sometimes at church could have lured me into thinking I was never going to be anything in life. As friends, family, and loved ones, we need to begin speaking life, love, and encouragement into those we say we care about.

What you feed the mind is what you become; what you starve will normally die. So, if you choose to abort all the negative darts that are thrown your way, your mind will have time to speak the truth to you, and help you move from what I consider your own prison sentence. Whatsoever a man thinks is what he is, so speak hope, peace, joy, success, and prosperity to yourself and begin to walk in it. You are able to do anything you want to do.

This reminds me of a good friend of mine who spent over 17 years in prison on death row; I met her in the prison years ago. She would tell every prisoner she passed on the yard, "I am getting out of here one day."

They looked at her as if she were crazy; until one day the governor gave her a pardon to be released. When she got out, even to this day, I call her and say, "YOU ARE SOMEBODY," and then I hang up the phone. She has been on many TV shows and has appeared at many conferences. She has even spoken at Bishop Jakes *Woman Thou Art Loosed Conference*.

Is this because of me? NO! It's all because of what she thought about herself, and what she did not accept as her destiny. If she can speak herself off death row, by asking God to release her, then you too can speak yourself into another destiny. You don't have to settle for less when God has promised you the best.

CHAPTER 11

Entrapment, Exposure, & Entitlement

Entrapment is a sorry way of catching someone doing wrong. Entrapment is when you don't play by the set rules of the game, and you set out to conquer defeat or win the game by deception.

The legal definition for this word is...

[4]"In criminal law, entrapment is conduct by a law enforcement agent inducing a person to commit an offense that the person would otherwise have been unlikely to commit. [1] In many jurisdictions, entrapment is a possible defense against criminal liability. However, there is no entrapment where a person is ready and willing to break the law, and the government agents merely provide what appears to be a favorable opportunity for the person to commit the crime."

---

[4] https://en.wikipedia.org/wiki/Entrapment

Who would ever think our law enforcement agencies could operate in such a manner as this? For example, it is not entrapment for a government agent to pretend to be someone else and to offer, either directly, through an informant, or other decoy, to engage in an unlawful transaction with the person (see sting operation).

So, a person would not be a victim of entrapment if the other person was ready, willing, and able to commit the crime charged in the indictment at the time they offered the opportunity. Those government officers or agents did no more than offer an opportunity.

On the other hand, if the evidence leaves a reasonable doubt, whether the person had any intent to commit the crime had it not been for inducement or persuasion on the part of some government officer or agent, then the person is not guilty. For example, if a defendant had purchased illegal drugs from an undercover officer, he may be found not guilty if it is determined that the officer initiated the transaction or aggressively pressed the accused to complete it.

So, if this is the law of entrapment, why do so many officers get charged with entrapment? The reason for this charge is due to greedy law enforcement officers who will do anything to make their quota for the month. They will draw you into areas they know are dangerous for you. They lay back and wait for you to do wrong, even though they laid the trap.

This reminds me of some of our comedy shows like the Dukes of Hazzard, where the police officer would ride around with a speed limit sign in his trunk that posted a lower speed than the normal speed. He would drive up ahead of the Dukes and hang this sign before they got there and then pull them over for speeding. That is what you call entrapment.

This is just how the devil works against us as children of God. He carries scriptures in his trunk that he knows you have a problem obeying, and as soon as he gets an opportunity, he drives ahead of you on the road you are traveling and hangs those signs hoping that you would disobey God's laws. Why? Because he knows that God is the law keeper, and he understands that God does not play when it comes to the Words He speaks in this world as law.

Paul said in Romans 7, "For we know that the law is spiritual, for when there was no law, I thought I was free, but when the law was established, sin found an opportunity to find me guilty of the law."

In other words, as long as I don't know what I was doing was wrong, I was okay. But now that I know it isn't right, the devil has found a way to entrap me. Let's look closer at these written laws which define entrapment, and you will see how Satan works in every moment to justify these laws.

"Entrapment is the idea for committing the crime which came from the government agents, principalities in high places, even rulers of wickedness and not from the person accused of the crime."

Remember that older cousin that mom left to babysit you? And how they would suggest, "The cookies mom made would probably melt in your mouth, huh?"

They would say things that would excite your appetite without them telling you to go get one. They knew mom said not to touch them, but you were not there when she said it. They let you go to get one and then took a bite off yours, being able to say I did not tell them they could have one. They lured you into going against what mom said should not happen by exciting your taste buds and desires to have just one. Someone you trusted to be honest with you fooled and tricked you.

Sounds like the devil to me. He causes people to build this false trust in him, and then he lowers the boom on them when it's too late to turn and stop.

Entitlement

But thank God for the law of Entitlement, which operates on mercy and grace. David's two best friends were grace and mercy. David said, "Yea, though I walk through the valley and shadows of death I will not fear no evil, because thy rod and staff are there for me, and Grace and Mercy are following me all the days of my life." (Psalms 23:1)

David was assured that there would be many traps in his life, as he walked through the shadows of death, but he also was convinced in his walking with God that the shadows were only able to bring about fear, if he allowed them to. David recognized that fear and giving into it was a choice.

When you know that God has entitled you with power that rules over all death, hell, and the grave, you walk in power, love, and a sound mind. This is what Paul was sharing with

Timothy, as he encouraged him not to let himself get trapped by the issues people had with him. However, Timothy had to stand on the fact that he was entitled to the position he was put in.

The people were trying to influence him to stop because of his age; they wanted him to accept that he was not able to do the job effectively, and that Paul did not prepare him for this task. They were treating Timothy about how most churches today treat younger pastors. "Sit down and learn some more," as they tell them.

They will make you feel you are still wet behind the ears, milk on your breath, and you don't have enough wisdom to rule over them. When you allow the foolishness of man's speaking negatively to lure you into their trap, you find it hard to get free from them.

John 11:44 Jesus said, "Loose him and Let him go." Mary and Martha, along with the people, would not loose him from his grave clothes; some felt he should still be dead even after Jesus had spoken life and freedom into him. When you know you are entitled to fairness, you don't worry about being entrapped, you just focus in on the exposure of the trickster.

Exposure of the Enemy

Just as the officer is called to the table by his commanding officer, so is the enemy when he is caught in his no-good antics. There was a day when God was meeting with the angels Job said, and God saw Satan when he showed up and God the Father stopped the meeting and asked him, "Why are you here and what have you been doing outside of my courts?"

The Devil was exposed at that very moment as he had to give an account of his whereabouts. He said I busted, "I have been out seeking to and from for those who are dry, and those I can devour."

He understood that when God saw him creeping, he would be brought to the table. It was Colossians where we see Jesus shame the Devil openly.

Devil Exposed

He disarmed the rulers and authorities (And having spoiled principalities and powers; he made a show of them openly. Principalities of hell, the infernal powers of darkness, the devil that had them) **and put them to open shame, triumphing over them in him** (in and by his Son Jesus Christ).

Colossians 2:15 ESV

(emphasis author's)

There were many occasions where Jesus had to expose the Devil's spirit in some of those he came in contact with. Peter and John, in the book of Acts, told the woman to be quiet, who was trying to tell the Gentile people who Jesus really was, way before the appointed time. Peter told that spirit in the woman to shut-up and hold its peace.

Scripture Proof

Matthew 8:24 ESV — Have you come here to torture us before the appointed time?... The time is not yet come, for the dissolution of our empire and government in the Gentile world?

Luke 4:34 NIV — Our business should be to spread abroad Christ's fame in every place, to beseech him in behalf... Have you come here to torture us before the appointed time?

Mark 1:24 KJV — Saying, Let us alone; what have we to do

with thee, thou Jesus of Nazareth? Art thou come to destroy us? I know you and who thou art, the Holy One of God...

Be Aware

We all can see that Jesus has no problem exposing the devil at his game. Satan understands that our Father does not play; he knows that God is a lover of His children, and He goes to and from in the strength of the believers. We don't have time to keep falling into the same traps, over and over again. There comes a time in life when we, as children of God, will have to be aware of every scheme Satan throws out to make us disobey God's law.

"You did run well, but who hindered you that you would not obey the truth anymore?"

Galatians 5:7

There is a story in Zachariah, where the prophet is having a vision of the Lord and Joshua the High Priest talking. The Bible says that Satan shows up and is standing on the right-hand side of Joshua, ready to accuse him.

Isn't that just like the devil, always trying to trap you and make us look bad before God's presence? I love this particular vision of Zachariah, because it allows us to see how God protects His own when Satan is constantly trying to bring accusations.

Scripture says that Satan was accusing Joshua of having dirty garments on before God. Well, to the natural eye, you would ask, "What does Joshua's clothing have to do with anything?"

They have a whole lot to do with this passage of scripture. The number one reason Satan had the right to bring up a case against the prophet is because the Mosaic Law stated that a High Priest was to never come before the presence of God with a filthy garment on. That's why even to this day, the Jewish Rabbi, and High Officials, still change clothes multiple times in ceremonial services.

It is within all rights for them to be clean when ministering in the Holy Place. For it was a custom that if a high priest went into the most holy place without clean garments, they would drop dead in the very presence of God.

So, for the safety of the other priests that were working in the temple, they would tie a rope with bells around the high priest's waist. They knew that as long as the bells were ringing and there was movement, then the priest was okay. But once those bills stopped ringing and there was no more movement of the rope, those who were outside working in the Tabernacle would pull the rope and pull the high priest out, because he had dropped dead in the presence of God.

This is the accusation that Satan was bringing against Joshua. He felt if others would drop dead in the presence of God, why was it that Joshua was still standing before God with dirty garments on? You really have to know the schemes and the wiles of the devil to see what he was up to at this time.

He knows the bible, he knows scripture, he knows the word from Genesis to Revelation. We must remember that it was the word that Satan used, even against our Lord and Savior, Jesus Christ, to test Him and to tempt Him after 40 days of fasting in the wilderness.

But God's response is phenomenal. He looks at Lucifer and says to him, "The Lord rebuke you! Was this not one of mine who was plucked out of the fire of Israel?"

In other words, what He was telling the devil is that *he would not be dirty if the dirt that's on his garments did not come from you.*

Secondly, God was allowing the people to understand that this was a high priest who was doing the work of ministry in the Tabernacle. There is no way possible that you can do all the sacrifices that were made in the Tabernacle and not get blood, dirt, feces, dung, and other kinds of secretions all over your Sacred Vestments.

There is one thing that the devil forgets when he tries to accuse you or accuse us before God. It's not the error of the person that God looks at, but it is the heart.

See, Satan thought that what was being portrayed on the outside would be the end of the relationship between God and Joshua. But God showed Satan openly that He was not looking at the outer appearance of man.

Watch what he does!

He orders the angels that are there to bring Joshua a set of clean garments and place them upon Joshua in the very presence of his accuser, Satan himself. Not only does He order for a new garment to be brought, but He orders the old dirty stuff to be taken off in front of the one who is the father of dirt, father of lies, manipulation, and deception.

And God, being who He is, doesn't stop with just the garments that he wore on his body, God also asks for a new turban to be brought in and placed on the head of Joshua, which represents the service of ministry that he will be moving forward into, even though his enemy was there trying to make him look bad.

As you now know, it is against the law to be entrapped by someone of authority. And no matter how much the devil tries to entrap you, no matter how much he tries to enforce his entanglements of bondage in your life, we are responsible to maintain our focus on God.

RESOLVED: It really should not matter what Satan brings you away. What matters to God is how you respond to his foolish tactics.

Yes, there may have been sometimes where Satan has trapped you in his web and entangled you with his foolishness. But keep in mind, your time with him has never been permanent.

If you would just seek the Lord while he may be found, come call you upon him while he is near, forsake your ways, and your thoughts, and return unto the Lord. The Bible says he would abundantly pardon us.

What is a pardon? A pardon can be given to you as a prisoner on death row at the very minute before 12:00 by the governor. But even if the government gives a written document or statement saying you are able to stay alive, the written document is not valid until you, yourself, sign it at the bottom.

What I'm trying to tell you today is that God has set us free from the entanglements, from the bondages, from the tricks, from the traumas, from the trials that the devil has brought our way. But when you give your life to Christ Jesus, you sign on the dotted lines to say I am receiving the pardon that my Lord and Savior gave me on Calvary's Cross.

Remember, you don't have to be entangled with the yoke of bondage ever again in your life. For the Bible tells us to be not entangled with the yoke of bondage, the freedom of God has made you free, after you have done all to stand, stand!

Stand for right, stand for God, stand for the Lord Jesus Christ, stand for the Salvation that has been given to us, and stand for the resurrection that sealed the whole deal.

If you look back at the life of Steven, who was the very first martyr for Christ's sake, you will see Jesus standing on the right side of the Father, ready to assist and welcome Steven home.

What I'm trying to say to you today in this resolve is that if you stand up for God, He will surely stand up for you. God bless.

PRAYER: Dear God, I pray you would show yourself strong in the lives of these readers. Lord, I believe for them that you can do exceedingly, abundantly more than we could ever ask or think. Thank you in advance, Father, for giving us your son to set us free.

Amen!

www.ingramcontent.com/pod-product-compliance
Lightning Source LLC
Chambersburg PA
CBHW072155090426
42740CB00012B/2279